WHAT A DIFFERENCE A NAME MAKES

A Practical Guide For a Study of The Name Yahweh

Jim & Val Harvey

CROSSBOOKS
PUBLISHING

CrossBooks™
A Division of LifeWay
1663 Liberty Drive
Bloomington, IN 47403
www.crossbooks.com
Phone: 1-866-879-0502

First published by CrossBooks 7/26/2011

ISBN: 978-1-4627-0531-3 (sc)
ISBN: 978-1-4627-0532-0 (hc)

Library of Congress Control Number: 2011935162

Printed in the United States of America

This book is printed on acid-free paper.

Dedicated to our dear family and all those friends
who have made our lives so meaningful.

CONTENTS

PREFACE

THIS BOOK IS A sequel to *Who Changed God's Name?* The thesis of the previous book was that *Yahweh* is the original name for God. Moses received the revelation of that name at the burning bush described in Exodus 3:1—4:17. Subsequently, this name occurs 6,828 times in the Old Testament, and was changed by various Bible translators to *Jehovah* and *LORD*. These terms fail to convey the true meaning of God's name.

The response of many readers to the first book has been extremely gratifying. One friend wrote, "My mother and I have been reading your book together as part of our daily Bible study. We were not previously familiar with the many combinations using Yahweh's name and how they indicate that He is all we need to become all He wants us to be. This understanding has changed the way we pray and deepened our faith for sure."

A missionary in Rwanda, Africa, obtained the book and said: "My husband and I have been on the mission field in Africa for two years, and honestly, I am exhausted. We read your statement that Yahweh means, 'I AM whatever you need in order to become all that I want you to be.' I had known this truth in my head, but not until now do I understand it in my heart. This book has cleared up much confusion for me and yet it is so basic. Bless you for proclaiming His greatness."

My friends Alan and Tina Lyle are missionaries in Rome, Italy. He shared this testimony: "Recently, I took your book along with me on my way to meet a new contact. I was reading the book when he arrived. In our conversation he told me how he had so many needs in his life and was having trouble believing in Jesus. I opened the book and began showing him all the combination names you had listed and that each one revealed how God could meet various needs. As he looked over those terms, he realized that this was true and all he needed to do was to believe. I hope you will find it encouraging to know that while you were writing this book, God was preparing Sorin to receive these truths and be saved."

Many other similar responses have caused us to realize that **Yahweh is working to reveal truth about Himself.** The failure of translators to accurately render His Name has concealed this truth. What has been lost by these mistranslations is the meaning of the most significant of all names—God's Name. This sequel is an attempt to restore to our understanding the importance of knowing God's Name. Help also is provided for claiming the amazing benefits that can come to those who call upon that Name. We have included many accounts of persons who have been transformed by Yahweh. **Our belief is that we all need the differences that only Yahweh can and will make.** Much of what appears in our first book on this subject is repeated here, however, we urge you to read that volume in addition to this one. (*Who Changed God's Name?* is available at www. Crossbooks.com)

INTRODUCTION

OUR FRIEND, JOHNNIE GODWIN, told us about an occasion when he was asked to introduce to an audience the well-known speaker, Elton Trueblood. Before the meeting, Johnnie said to him, "I look forward to hearing your speech." The wise leader replied, "I did not come to make a speech but to make a difference!"

We want to borrow that statement; we did not write just to make another book. We wrote to make a difference. Our plan is to accomplish this worthy goal by showing what a difference Yahweh has made and can continue making in every person.

My personal testimony confirms this. I became aware of God's name through my preparation to teach a college course entitled, "The History of the Israelite People." This study caused me to pursue biblical information on this special name. I discovered ten combinations of *Yahweh* with other Hebrew terms. The fact that the name Jesus comes from a Hebrew word *Yeshua* (or *Yesu*) meaning "Yahweh is salvation" further challenged me. Thus, closely related to the name Yahweh are the various claims Jesus made when He said, "I am the Bread of Life," "I am the Light of the World," "I am the Vine," "I am the Way, the Truth, and the Life," "I am the Resurrection and the Life," plus several others to be considered in this book.

These truths combined to give me a new insight into the nature of God. The Old Testament references to "LORD" suddenly became full of new meaning. That term should be *Yahweh*, the One who IS, and the One who takes the initiative in making covenant relationships with His people. Now as I read the Bible, I substitute "Yahweh" for "LORD" and reflect on what He is seeking to communicate to me in the context of this particular passage. Thus I find a far richer meaning to Bible study.

My attempts to know God—as Father, Son, and Holy Spirit, have a new life and vitality that was previously unknown to me. Now I understand more fully what He wants to mean to everyone and how He is committed to meeting all our needs in an abundant manner.

Prayer also has taken on new meaning. For example, when praying in private, I address God as Yahweh because this is His Name! When meditating on Him, I often think through all ten Old Testament combinations of His Name, plus all the I AM claims of Yeshua in the New Testament. Each of these reveals truth about Him that remains unknown to most worshipers. When I intercede in prayer for those who have illness, I pray in the name of Yahweh Rophe ("I AM the One who heals."). As I ask for guidance in making decisions, I pray in the name of Yahweh Rohi ("I AM the Good Shepherd.").

As we journey through each chapter of this book, perhaps you will understand as never before what a difference a name makes—the right name. All the truths we share in the following chapters find their source in the Bible—God's Word. We firmly believe that the Bible is the most valuable possession we will ever hold in our hands. **Yahweh has chosen to reveal Himself most clearly through the pages of His inspired Word.** As the psalmist declared, "Your word is a lamp for my feet and a light on my path" (Psalm 119:105) and, "The revelation of Your words brings light and gives understanding to the inexperienced" (Psalm 119:130).

Years ago I came across a very meaningful biblical statement that summarizes what God intends for His Word to be for us. Listen to these words through the pen of the inspired apostle Paul: "For whatever was written before was written for our instruction, so that through our endurance and through the encouragement of the Scriptures we may have hope" (Romans 15:4). Paul was referring to his Scripture at that time—the Old Testament. The same truth applies to our Bible—both testaments. All the Scripture has come to us as a special gift from God. This gift instructs us in such a manner that, regardless of our circumstances, "we may have hope."

The hope of knowing God more intimately and of actually experiencing the radical difference He wants to make in us is made

far more possible by the understanding of His Name—who He is. This hope is *What a Difference a Name Makes* is all about.

We want to recommend a special Bible translation to you: *The HCSB Study Bible* (2010). This Bible is a revised version of *The Holman Christian Standard Bible* (1999). The name *Yahweh* occurs over 600 times in the Old Testament of this translation. We applaud those who have taken a bold step in making this information available for the first time. We will all be blessed to read this more accurate translation.

Please join us in a journey of getting better acquainted with God through His real Name. May we not only be helped by this experience but also become effective witnesses to others of this amazing difference—The Difference a Name Can Make.

SUGGESTIONS FOR THE USE OF THE STUDY GUIDE

This book contains thirteen chapters. The design provides weekly resources for groups that follow Bible studies based on a three-month (one quarter) plan.

Each chapter concludes with a study guide based on the material in that chapter. These guides may be used by an individual or small group study.

Teachers who lead studies in a retreat setting or Bible conference could also adapt this material for that purpose.

All Scripture quotations are from the Holman Christian Standard Bible unless otherwise indicated. Study leaders who prefer other translations may substitute those works as appropriate.

The first book in this series, *Who Changed God's Name?* (CrossBooks) is recommended as a resource.

CHAPTER ONE

WHAT IS THIS NAME THAT MAKES A DIFFERENCE?

The Difference Between Tradition and Truth

YAHWEH
(YAH-way)

S EVERAL MONTHS AGO I called a pastor friend in another state. When the receptionist answered the phone, I asked to speak to Pastor Ron. She replied, "May I tell him who is calling?" Remembering the pastor's sense of humor and our long time friendship, I lowered my voice, and using my best North Carolina accent, I said, "This is Billy Graham." After a rather long pause, my friend answered in his most sanctimonious voice, "Hello, Dr. Graham, this is Pastor Ron." When I stopped laughing, I said, "Ron, this is Jim Harvey." Then he laughed and said, "You rascal; you certainly had us fooled. My receptionist and three staff members are standing here at my desk, anxiously waiting to see why Billy Graham is calling me!"

Names make a difference. **Names represent individuals, therefore the name of a special person has a special meaning to us.** In biblical times names were much more significant than today. Parents often gave names to their children that expressed a particular hope they had for this child. *The Holman Bible Dictionary* states, "The biblical concept of naming was rooted in the ancient world's understanding that a name expressed essence. To know the name of a person was to know that person's total character and nature...The knowing of a name implied a relationship

1

between parties in which power to do harm or good was in force" (p. 1007).

When we read someone's name in the Bible, it is just another name to us. But to those first readers most names revealed something significant about that individual. For example, the name *David* means "beloved," and you may remember that he became the only person in the Bible of whom the Lord said, "He is a man after My heart" (Acts 13:22). How very beloved he was. *Samson* means "strong." *Adam* means "mankind," *Eve* means "life."

Sometimes a biblical person's name was altered to reflect a change in them or in their place in God's plan. *Jacob* ("a deceiver or cheater") became *Israel* ("God rules"). Abram's name ("father is exalted") was changed to *Abraham* ("father of a multitude"). He became the original father of all Arabs and Jews. Barnabas ("Son of Encouragement") was the name given by the apostles to a man named Joseph (Acts 4:36). Many references to him are found in Acts and Paul's letters. Most of the time, Barnabas was encouraging others.

The list of such examples could go on and on, but these are adequate to demonstrate the importance of someone's name in biblical times. Not only was the meaning of a person's name significant but also knowing that name often gave privileged access to that person. The same is true today. For example, if you call a business firm and want to speak to a person of influence, it helps if you can ask for that individual by name—you have better access to them than if you simply asked to speak to "the manager."

Now, let's apply these truths about names to the name of the most important of all persons—God. The fact that biblical names often had significant meanings has been pointed out. Names revealed the essential character of a person, and provided privileged access to that person. What does this tell us about God's name?

First, **the fact that God took the initiative in making known His name is a matter of remarkable importance.** By giving His name to Moses, God was expressing the fact that He wants to be known and to be accessible to humankind, even to sinners like Moses and everyone else. Let me remind you of this very amazing encounter.

God's Name Revealed

Moses was the man God chose to lead His people out of bondage in Egypt. He had been exiled from Egypt, living in the desert for forty years when this life-changing incident occurred as recorded personally by Moses. Notice his testimony as recorded in the book of Exodus.

"Meanwhile Moses was shepherding the flock of his father-in-law Jethro, the priest of Midian. He led the flock to the far side of the wilderness and came to Horeb, the mountain of God. Then the Angel of the LORD appeared to him in a flame of fire within bush. As Moses looked, he saw that the bush was on fire but was not consumed. So Moses thought: I must go over and look at the remarkable sight. Why isn't the bush burning up?

When the LORD saw that he had gone over to look, God called out to him from the bush, "Moses, Moses!" "Here I am," he answered. "Do not come closer," He said. "Take your sandals off your feet, for the place where you are standing is holy ground." Then He continued, "I am the God of your father, the God of Abraham, the God of Isaac, and the God of Jacob." Moses hid his face because he was afraid to look at God.

Then the LORD said, "I have observed the misery of My people in Egypt, and have heard them crying out because of their oppressors, and I know about their sufferings. I have come down to rescue them from the power of the Egyptians and to bring them from that land to a good and spacious land, a land flowing with milk and honey—the territory of the Canaanites, Hittites, Amorites, Perizzites, Hivites, and Jebusites. The Israelites cry for help has come to Me, and I also have seen the way the Egyptians are oppressing them. Therefore, go. I am sending you to Pharaoh so that you may lead My people, the Israelites, out of Egypt."

But Moses asked God, "Who am I that I should go to Pharaoh and that I should bring the Israelites out of Egypt?" He answered, "I will certainly be with you, and this will be the sign to you that I have send you: when you bring the people out of Egypt, you will all worship God at this mountain."

Then Moses asked God, "If I go to the Israelites and say to them: The God of your fathers has sent me to you, and they ask me, 'What is His name?' what should I tell them?" God replied to Moses, "I AM WHO I AM. This is what you are to say to the Israelites: I AM has sent me to you." God also said to Moses, "Say this to the Israelites: **Yahweh,** the God of your fathers, the God of Abraham, the God of Isaac, and the God of Jacob, has sent me to you. **This is My name forever; this is how I am to be remembered in every generation.**

"Go and assemble the elders of Israel and say to them: **Yahweh,** the God of your fathers, the God of Abraham, Isaac, and Jacob has appeared to me..." (Exodus 3:1-16).

Moses obeyed the LORD and returned to Egypt where he confronted Pharaoh, telling him about his God-given mission to lead the Israelites out of Egypt. Pharaoh responded by making life for the Israelites even more miserable. When Moses returned to the LORD with this disturbing news, the LORD replied,

"I am Yahweh. I appeared to Abraham, Isaac, and Jacob as God Almighty, but **I did not make My name Yahweh known to them.** I also established My covenant with them to give them the land of Canaan, the land they lived in as foreigners. Furthermore, I have heard the groaning of the Israelites, whom the Egyptians are forcing to work as slaves, and I have remembered my covenant. Therefore tell the Israelites: **I am Yahweh,** and I will deliver you from the forced labor of the Egyptians and free you from slavery to them...**You will know that I am Yahweh your God,** who delivered you from the forced labor of the Egyptians" (Exodus 6:2-7). [Words in bold type supplied by the author.]

[English translations of the Bible that use the word "Yahweh" in this passage include: New Jerusalem Bible (1985), Amplified Bible (1987), New Living Translation (2007), English Standard Version (2001), Holman Christian Standard Bible (2004), and World English Bible (in process).]

What is God's name? God Himself answers this question in the words we have just read: **"My name is Yahweh...this is how I am to be remembered in every generation."** Why do you suppose God chose this particular name for Himself? What does *Yahweh* mean? Hebrew is the original language

"My name is Yahweh... this is how I am to be remembered in every generation."

4

for nearly the entire Old Testament. We believe Moses recorded this conversation with God in his native Hebrew language. One unusual feature of the Hebrew language is that it is written in consonants, with no vowels. The Hebrew people learned to read their language without vowels, and then learned to supply the necessary vowels as they spoke the words.

Yahweh is composed of four Hebrew consonants יהוה. In English these translate to YHWH. Scholars refer to these words as the *Tetragrammaton*, a word from the Greek language meaning "four letters." **Yahweh is found 6,828 times in the Old Testament,** occurring in every book except Esther, Ecclesiastes, and the Song of Solomon.

The third of the Ten Commandments warned the Hebrews not to misuse God's name: "Do not misuse the name of Yahweh your God, because Yahweh will punish anyone who misuses His name" (Exodus 20:7). The response of Hebrew people was to refrain from ever speaking His name, just to make sure they did not disobey God. In the Middle Ages the scribes used a clever method of making certain God's name was not pronounced. Each time the four consonants YHWH occurred, they inserted the vowels used to pronounce *adonai,* a Hebrew word translated "Lord." Thus when they came to *YHWH* in reading they were reminded to pronounce the substitute word "Lord" rather than "Yahweh." Later, English translators expressed these two different words by using upper case letters for **Yahweh—"LORD,"** and lower case letters for ***adonai*—"Lord."**

As a result of this attempt to give special respect to God's name, no pronunciation of this sacred word existed for hundreds of years. Thus no one today knows for certain how to pronounce YHWH. However, most scholars, from the study of the structure of the Hebrew language, believe the best pronunciation is Yahweh (YAH-way).

One very unfortunate development has occurred with reference to God's name. The Encyclopedia Britannica states: "Yahweh—the personal name of the God of the Israelites. . . .The Massoretes, Jewish biblical scholars of the Middle Ages, replaced the vowel signs that had appeared above or beneath the consonants of YHWH with the vowel signs of Adonai or Elohim. **Thus the artificial name of Jehovah** (YeHoWaH) came into being. Although Christian scholars after the Renaissance and the Reformation periods used the term Jehovah for YHWH, in the 19th and 20th centuries biblical scholars began to use the form Yahweh again, thus this pronunciation of the Tetragrammaton was never really lost. Greek transcriptions also indicate the YHWH should be pronounced Yahweh." (Encyclopedia Britannica, [15th edition] vol. 10, "Yahweh," p. 786)

Today the use of *Jehovah* for God's name is very common. The King James Version of the Bible is responsible for most of these references. There are seven verses where the KJV uses Jehovah in place of Yahweh. The remaining 6,821 occurrences of *Yahweh* are translated as "LORD." Notice this statement in the quotation above: "Thus the artificial name of Jehovah came into being." **There is no Hebrew word for Jehovah, this term is a hybrid (artificial) word made up from the consonants of YHWH and the vowels of adonai. Jehovah, as a word, has no meaning**. What a shame that the name of the most important person in this universe should be rendered by a word that has no meaning!

But what about the other 6,821 occurrences of YHWH that are expressed in most English translations as "LORD," a word that means "sovereign one"? Whether this word is spelled LORD or Lord, the meaning is the same, and is not the meaning of YHWH—God's name. So what does His name mean?

God's Name Defined

When Moses asked God to reveal His name, God replied, "I AM WHO I AM. This is what you are to say to the Israelites: I AM has sent me to you" (Exodus 3:14). The name *Yahweh* comes from the Hebrew verb meaning "to be." **God was revealing Himself as the God WHO IS—the only living God, in contrast to all the false gods who ARE NOT!**

Furthermore, He was declaring that He always has been and always will be—He is eternal! Time, as we understand it, does not apply to God. He is beyond time. From eternity past to eternity future (as we think of time) God IS. He always has been and always will be—I AM. Notice that God said to Moses, "Yahweh, the God of your fathers, the God of Abraham, the God of Isaac, and the God of Jacob...this is My name forever; this is how I am to be remembered in every generation" (Exodus 3:14). When Yahweh said, "every generation," He certainly included our generation. He desires that we know Him as *Yahweh* (I AM).

This truth has important implications for us. Although we read about God's actions in the past, and His promises regarding the future, He wants us to think of Him, not as I WAS or as I WILL BE, but as I AM—the One who is present right now! He was making this very clear to Moses, an eighty-year old shepherd.

Can you imagine how totally unqualified and incapable Moses felt when this voice spoke to him from a burning bush, saying to him, "I am sending you to Pharaoh so that you may lead My people, the Israelites, out of Egypt"?

Moses' initial response was to convince God that He had made a mistake. He gave God some "what ifs"—what if they won't believe me; what if they won't obey me? So God performed several miracles as signs that He would be with him. Still, Moses tried to beg off by saying he couldn't speak well; God replied that He would help him and teach him what to say. Finally, in desperation, Moses said, "Please, Yahweh, send someone else" (Exodus 4:13).

God's first revelation of Himself as *Yahweh* was to this reluctant man. He wanted to assure him, as he faced an incredibly difficult assignment, that God would be whatever he needed. Through this special name *Yahweh,* God was saying to Moses and to us, **I AM WHATEVER YOU NEED IN ORDER TO BE AND DO WHATEVER I WANT OF YOU!**

God also was revealing Himself as One who takes the initiative in making covenants with His people. His first covenant with Israel was the one He made with Abraham when He promised, "I will make you into a great nation, I will bless you, I will make your name great, and you will be a blessing…all the peoples on earth will be blessed through you…I will give this land to your offspring" (Genesis 12:2-3, 7).

Hundreds of years later Yahweh appeared to Moses at the burning bush to remind him of this ancient promise, and to renew the covenant blessing. ***Yahweh* is God's covenant name.** Read once more this promise: "God spoke to Moses telling him, 'I am **Yahweh**. I appeared to Abraham, Isaac, and Jacob as God Almighty, but I did not make My name **Yahweh** known to them…I have remembered My covenant.'" (Exodus 6: 2-5).

The meaning of *Yahweh* might well be summarized by saying **this name speaks of God's *presence* and His *promises*;** He is always with us and always faithful to all His promises to us. Can you see why He chose this name and why He wants us to know this very meaningful, significant name? For this reason, I say the translators of the English Bible have often failed to accurately render God's name. How many readers of the Bible will comprehend all God intends to convey by His name if we read "LORD," rather than "Yahweh"?

One example of what I mean is found in Psalm 8. The chapter begins with this prayer: "LORD, our Lord, how magnificent is Your name throughout the earth!" How many readers know that "LORD" in the original text is actually "Yahweh," while the second "Lord" is an accurate translation of the word meaning "sovereign one"? These words express a prayer of praise to Yahweh for His "magnificent" name, and yet, His name (Yahweh) is not given, instead a substitute word "LORD" that does not convey anything about the true meaning of His name! What a loss; what a sad mistranslation!

God's Son's Name

Proverbs 30 begins with a series of questions attributed to a man named Agur. Nothing is known about this man other than what is said in verse 1: "The words of Agur son of Jakeh." However, Agur asks some very interesting questions: "Who has gone up to heaven and come down? Who has gathered the wind in His hands? Who has bound up the waters in a cloak? Who has established all the ends of the earth?" (Proverbs 30:4). The most reasonable answer to these questions is *God*. Now, notice the next question: "What is His name, and what is the name of His Son—if you know?"

We have just considered God's name—*Yahweh*. Let's turn our attention to Yahweh's Son's name. As Agur asked, "What is the name of His Son?" From all four gospel accounts, we know that **Jesus** is the only begotten Son of God. **The name *Jesus* is an English translation of the Greek word *Iesous*, which in turn translates the Hebrew name *Yeshua* (or *Yesu*), meaning "Yahweh the Savior" or "Yahweh is salvation."** You may remember that before Jesus was born, an angel appeared to Joseph in a dream saying. "Joseph, son of David, don't be afraid to take Mary as your wife, because what has been conceived in her is by

> *The name Jesus is an English translation of the Greek word Iesous, which in turn translates the Hebrew name Yeshua (or Yesu), meaning "Yahweh the Savior" or "Yahweh is salvation."*

the Holy Spirit. She will give birth to a son, and you are to name Him Jesus, because He will save His people from their sins" (Matthew 1: 20-21).

We see that Yahweh's Son's name is Jesus (in Greek, *Iesous*; in Hebrew, *Yeshua*) **which means "Yahweh saves."** Another very important word must be added to Jesus' name, and that is, *Christ*. He is Jesus Christ. This word comes from another Hebrew word *Messiah* meaning "anointed one." *Jesus* is His personal name; *Christ* is His title. The first announcement of this truth is found in Andrew's words to his brother Simon: "We have found the Messiah! [which means *Anointed One*], and he brought Simon to Jesus" (John 1:41-42).

Throughout the Old Testament prophesies was the promise that Yahweh would send the Messiah (Christ) to deliver His people and establish His kingdom on earth. Jesus is the fulfillment of all these promises. The name *Jesus* occurs over 700 times in the New Testament. **Since His name means "Yahweh saves,"** *Yahweh* **is found more than 7,500 times in God's Word! Amazing!**

God's Name Exalted

Some time ago I used a Bible concordance to see how many references there are to "the name of the LORD [Yahweh]." I discovered over 500 such occurrences. What a powerful testimony to the prominence God gives to His name. One scholar made this statement: "The expression 'name of God' designates at the same time the whole divine self-presentation by which God in personal presence testifies of Himself—the whole side of the divine nature which is turned toward man" [Gustov F. Oehler, *Theology of the Old Testament*, p. 125].

Follow this guide through a few of these references; notice they come from all portions of the Bible.

OLD TESTAMENT

Genesis 4:26 "A son was born to Seth also, and he named him Enosh. At that time people began to call on the name of Yahweh."

Exodus 34:5 "And Yahweh came down in a cloud, stood with him there, and proclaimed His name Yahweh."

Leviticus 22:2 "Tell Aaron and his sons to deal respectfully with the holy offerings of the Israelites that they have consecrated to Me, so they do not profane My holy name; I am Yahweh."

Numbers 6:27 "In this way they will put My name on the Israelites, and I will bless them."

Deuteronomy 32:3 "For I will proclaim Yahweh's name. Declare the greatness of our God."

Joshua 9:9 "Your servants have come from a far away land because of the name of Yahweh your God."

1 Samuel 17:45 "I come against you in the name of Yahweh of hosts, the God of Israel's armies."

1 Kings 18:24 "I will call on the name of Yahweh."

1 Chronicles 16:2 "When David had finished offering the burnt offerings and the fellowship offerings, he blessed the people in the name of Yahweh."

Job 1:21 "Yahweh gives, and Yahweh takes away. Praise the name of Yahweh."

Psalm 102:15 "Then the nations will fear the name of Yahweh."

Proverbs 18:10 "The name of Yahweh is a strong tower."

Isaiah 42:8 "I am Yahweh, that is My name."

Jeremiah 16:21 "They will know that My name is Yahweh."

Ezekiel 39:7 "So I will make My holy name known among My people Israel and will no longer allow it to be profaned. Then the nations will know that I am Yahweh, the Holy One in Israel."

Joel 2:32 "Then everyone who calls on the name of Yahweh will be saved."

Malachi 1:11 " My name will be great among the nations says Yahweh of hosts."

NEW TESTAMENT

Matthew 21:9 "Hosanna to the Son of David! Blessed is He who comes in the name of Yahweh!"

Mark 9:37 "Whoever welcomes one little child such as this in My name welcomes Me."

Luke 13:35 "You will not see Me until the time comes when you say, 'Blessed is He who comes in <u>the name of Yahweh</u>.'"

John 16:23 "I assure you: Anything you ask the Father <u>in My name</u>, He will give you."

Acts 2:21 "Whoever calls on <u>the name of Yahweh</u> will be saved."

Romans 9:17 "For this reason I raised you up; so that I may display My power in you, and that <u>My name</u> may be proclaimed in all the earth."

1 Corinthians 6:11 "You were justified in <u>the name of the Lord Yeshua</u> Christ and by the Spirit of our God."

Philippians 2: 9-11 "For this reason God also highly exalted Him and gave Him the name that is above every name, so that at <u>the name of Yeshua</u> every knee should bow...."

Colossians 3:17 "And whatever you do, in word or in deed, do everything in <u>the name of the Lord Yeshua</u>, giving thanks to God the Father through Him."

James 5:10 "Brothers, take the prophets who spoke <u>in Yahweh's name</u> as an example of suffering and patience."

Revelation 2:13 "I know where you live—where Satan's throne is! And you are holding on <u>to My name</u>."

My reason for listing these references (and there are hundreds of others) is to **demonstrate the obvious manner in which biblical writers were inspired to magnify the importance of God's name. His name represents Him--His nature and character, His purpose and power— in a very unique and significant manner.** Therefore we must not only know His name but refer to that name as His word declares. I agree with others who say that we are not required to know the original languages of the Scriptures—Hebrew, Aramaic, and Greek—in order to understand its true message and intent. However, I am insisting that those languages be translated accurately into English, or whatever language a reader understands.

For this reason I am upholding the use of *Yahweh*, rather than *LORD* for accurate biblical studies and teaching. ***Yahweh* is the English translation of His Hebrew name (YHWH), while *LORD* is not a translation but a title that is substituted for His name.**

Consider this latter point in this way: I have one name—James Earl Harvey; that's it. However, I have several titles that family and friends often use in reference to me, such as Dad, Father, Husband, Son, Grandfather, Pastor, Teacher, Professor, Friend, and so on. One name; many titles. Now let's apply this truth to God. In my library I have several books on the subject of "The Names of God." These authors give helpful information about various *titles* (not names) used in the Bible to describe God, such as, Lord, Father, God, Savior, Holy Spirit, Son, Almighty, Creator, Redeemer, King of kings, Lord of lords, and the list goes on. My point is that all these are important and very meaningful terms that help us understand more about God, but **none of these is His name!**

A friend recently sent this interesting quote from Max Lucado's book of devotionals: "*Yahweh* is God's name. You can call me preacher or writer or half-baked golfer—these are accurate descriptions, but these aren't my names. I might call you dad, mom, doctor, or student, and although those terms may describe you, they aren't your name. If you want to call me by name, say 'Max.' If I call you by your name, I say it. And if you want to call God by his name, say, 'Yahweh'." [*Traveling Light*, Max Lucado, p.13, Thomas Nelson]

Just like all of us, **God has one name: *Yahweh*.** The following are some of His own statements that we have just reviewed about His name:

Yahweh…. This is My name forever; this is how I am to be remembered in every generation (Exodus 3:15).

Then God spoke to Moses, telling him, "I am Yahweh. I appeared to Abraham, Isaac, and Jacob as God Almighty, but I did not make My name Yahweh known to them" (Exodus 6: 2-3).

I am Yahweh, that is My name (Isaiah 42:8).

Therefore, I am about to inform them, and this time I will make them know My power and My might; then they will know that My name is Yahweh (Jeremiah 16:21).

The subtitle of this chapter is "The Difference Between Tradition and Truth." A respected Bible scholar recently made this statement: "The most literal translation of the Hebrew name for God is *Yahweh*, but that is strange sounding to us, and *Jehovah* has come to posses a distinctive value we would be reluctant to forgo." Consider also this quote from a book written by a leader of the Jehovah's Witnesses sect: "While inclining to view the pronunciation 'Yahweh' as the more correct way, we have retained the form 'Jehovah' because of people's familiarity with it since the 14th century."

These two leaders base their choice of God's name on **tradition**—what translators and teachers have **traditionally** used for God's name for centuries—rather than biblical **truth**. I am saying that it is time to return to the original biblical name for God with all its intended revelation. **We conservative evangelicals insist on the absolute inerrancy and accuracy of the original manuscripts of the Bible. To be consistent with our professed belief in the authority of this Word, we must also insist on the most accurate translation of these inspired documents. Using** *Yahweh* **for God's name makes all the difference between tradition and truth!**

The following chapters of this book guide us in a study of numerous combinations of the name *Yahweh*. In addition are other Hebrew terms that add to God's revelation of who He is and what He wants to do for us. Welcome to this exciting adventure of learning the most important truths for our lives, both now and eternally.

Suggested prayer: **Father in heaven, thank You for choosing to reveal Yourself to us by giving us Your special name. Help us to understand all this name means. May we honor Your name by our use of this name and by our behavior as those who belong to You. Amen**

STUDY GUIDE

The questions are based on the thesis of this book—Knowing Yahweh makes a lasting difference in various aspects of a believers life.

Chapter One: The Difference Between Tradition and Truth

1. Underneath the following statements of tradition, express a contrasting truth.

    God cannot be known in the same way we know a friend.

    _____

    God has many names including Jehovah, LORD, Father, Master, and the Man Upstairs.

    _____

    God's real name is too sacred to be written or spoken.

    _____

2. Read Exodus 3:1-15 and list several significant happenings concerning Moses' interaction with God.

    a.

    b.

    c.

    What truth from verse 15 makes a difference in your understanding of God?

3.   What is the Hebrew background of the name Jesus?

4.   What have you discovered from Chapter One that helps you understand the difference between tradition and truth as it relates to God?

CHAPTER TWO

The Difference Between Our Poverty and God's Provision

YAHWEH YIREH
(YAH-way YI-rah)

O NE OF THE MOST remarkable and important events in the Bible is recorded—as an example for us—in Genesis 22. I emphasize "as an example for us" due to these words from the pen of the apostle Paul as he reminded his readers of Old Testament happenings: "Now these things became examples for us…." (1 Corinthians 10:6). In other words we should look upon the various events of biblical history as more than interesting occurrences. Our question should be: What can I learn from this scripture; is there some example here for me to follow?

Let's see what we can learn from this amazing story. You may recall how God called Abraham to be the beginning of a new nation of people, His chosen people—later known as *Israel* or the *Jews*. Obviously, all this possibility depended on Abraham having at least one son to be his heir. Genesis 18:1-15 relates the story of God promising to give a special son to Abraham and his wife Sarah in spite of their advanced ages. When Sarah heard about this promise, "she laughed to herself" (v. 12). How interesting that when this son was born, he was named Isaac, a name which means "laughter!"

All hope for Abraham becoming the father of a nation resided in this son, his only son. As Yahweh said to him, ". . . your offspring will be traced through Isaac" (Genesis 21:12). Thus we are surprised when Yahweh gave

16

Abraham this command, "Take your son, your only son Isaac, whom you love, go to the land of Moriah and offer him there as a burnt offering. . . ." (Genesis 22: 2). Fortunately, for our understanding, verse 1 reveals what Abraham did not know at the time. "God tested Abraham," with this strange request.

How commendable that, without any apparent questioning of God's plan in this matter, Abraham obeyed. The narrative continues as this man of faith got on his donkey, took Isaac along with two servants and wood for the burnt offering, a "fire," and a knife as they made a three-day journey to the appointed place of sacrifice. At this point, Abraham gave his servants these instructions: "Stay here with the donkey. The boy and I will go over there to worship; then we'll come back to you" (v. 5). Notice his words, "**we'll** come back to you." Abraham was confident that God would somehow bring Isaac through this experience alive!

Hundreds of years later, the writer of Hebrews called our attention to Abraham's faith in this situation: "By faith Abraham, when he was tested, offered up Isaac, he who had received the promises was offering up his unique son, about whom it had been said, 'In Isaac your seed will be called.' He considered God to be able even to raise someone from the dead, from which he also got him back as an illustration" (Hebrews 11:17-19).

As this father and son walked up the mountain, Isaac asked, "The fire and the wood are here, but where is the lamb for the burnt offering?" He had been with his father at previous times of worship and knew of the need for a sacrificial lamb. Listen to this expression of faith in Abraham's reply: "God himself will provide the lamb for the burnt offering, my son."

When they arrived at the appointed place, Abraham built the altar and put the wood in place. Then, to the surprise of Isaac, Abraham "bound his son Isaac and laid him on the altar, on top of the wood." Can you imagine what this father and son were thinking at this critical time? Obviously, Isaac was willing to submit to his father's actions. After all, Abraham was well over 100 years old. Isaac would probably have been a teenager or young man and could easily have overcome Abraham's attempt to bind him.

Several terms from this narrative add significance to what was happening. First, notice in verse 2 God described Isaac to Abraham as being, "your **only** son, whom you love." In fact, Isaac is described as the

17

"only son" three times in this passage. The point is: Abraham had no other son to be his heir and to carry on his hope of being the father of a special nation. By sacrificing Isaac, he was removing the possibility of seeing the fulfillment of Yahweh's promise to him (Genesis 17:1-9).

Moreover, Abraham **loved** his only son. Isaac was precious in his sight. Yahweh was testing Abraham's faith to see if he would obey the command to give up what he valued most highly—his only beloved son. All this must have been in this father's mind as he raised the knife to slay Isaac. This act would be like plunging a knife into his own heart!

And now for the rest of the story. At the last moment Abraham heard the voice of the Angel of Yahweh (obviously Yahweh Himself) telling him to stop the sacrifice, saying, "Now I know that you fear God, since you have not withheld you only son from Me" (v. 12). Abraham looked up and saw a ram caught by his horns in a nearby bush. Here was God's answer to Isaac's earlier question: "Where is the lamb?" Abraham proceeded to sacrifice this ram "in place of his son." What relief must have come to both Abraham and Isaac!

Abraham passed the test! His actions demonstrated the genuineness of his faith. Later, James used Abraham as an example of faith being "perfected" by works. He wrote: "Wasn't Abraham our father justified by works when he offered Isaac his son on the altar? You see that faith was active together with his works, and by works, faith was perfected" (James 2:21-22). **Yahweh tested Abraham to see if his professed faith was real—to see if he truly trusted Yahweh always to do what was best, even if he did not understand what was happening.** The answer to this amazing test, proven by his actions, was a resounding YES! In fact he could have said with Job, "Even if He kills me, I will hope in Him" (Job 13:15).

The One Who Provides

Following this episode Abraham gave a special name to the place where he had offered Isaac, he called it *Yahweh Yireh*, which in Hebrew means **"I AM the One who provides."** The word *Yireh l*iterally means "to see" and the word *provide* means "to see in advance." Yahweh saw in advance that a substitute would be needed in place of Isaac, so He provided a ram.

Notice the last part of this verse: "...so today it is said: 'It will be provided on Yahweh's mountain'" (Genesis 22:14). Let's give some thought to "Yahweh's mountain." We are told at the beginning of this chapter that this sacrifice was to be made on one of the mountains in the land of Moriah. Although Abraham had previously built altars and made sacrifices in other places, Yahweh insisted that the sacrifice of Isaac was to be at this special place—a place some thirty miles (three days journey) from Abraham's home in Beersheba. What was so special about this place?

This mountain became the location of Jerusalem and the temple. Notice these words: "Then Solomon began to build Yahweh's temple in Jerusalem on Mount Moriah where Yahweh had appeared to his father David" (2 Chronicles 3:1). For hundreds of years, thousands of animals were slain as sin offerings at the temple in Jerusalem—the same location where Abraham offered the ram in place of Isaac. On this same mountain God's only Son—the Son He loved—was offered as our sin offering on a cross. How interesting! How amazing!

Yahweh Yireh—God saw in advance that a perfect substitute was needed to die in our place, for our sin—and on this very same place, Jesus was offered for us. **The most needed provision Yahweh makes for us is an offering that satisfies His demands regarding our sin.** Why did God do this? Why make this provision that was so costly to Him? Why give His only begotten Son for such unworthy sinners as we? One word gives the answer: LOVE.

This leads to another very interesting and noteworthy fact about Genesis 22. A much respected conservative Bible interpreter, Henry M. Morris, wrote *The Genesis Record,* an excellent commentary on this first book of the Bible. He speaks about the "Principle of First Mention." Morris believes that "when an important word or concept appears in the Bible for the first time. . . the context in which it occurs sets the pattern for its primary usage and development all through the rest of Scripture" (p. 374).

One word that appears in Genesis 22 for the first time in the Bible is "love." Yahweh commanded Abraham, "Take your son . . . your only son whom you love, go to the land of Moriah and offer him there as a burnt offering . . . ." (22:2). The love of a father for his son is an appropriate example of the biblical meaning of true love. This fact is further expressed by the first occurrence of "love" in the New Testament. When Jesus was baptized, "There came a voice from heaven: This is My beloved Son. I take delight in Him!" (Matthew 3:17). Jesus spoke of this special kind of love in His prayer found in John 17 24: "Father…You loved Me before the world's foundation."

Now return to the question of why Yahweh Yireh provided His Son as a substitute on the cross for us. He loved us with this same fatherly love we have just read about. As Paul so eloquently states: "God proves His own love for us in that while we were still sinners Christ died for us" (Romans 5:8). And we must mention this familiar declaration: "For God loved the world in this way: He gave His One and Only Son, so that everyone who believes in Him will not perish but have eternal life" (John 3:16).

A second word that has its first Bible mention in Genesis 22 is "obey." Following Abraham's act of obedience in being willing to offer Isaac as a sacrifice, Yahweh spoke again to him. This time He renewed the same covenant made with Abraham many years before. He promises that Abraham would be blessed by having as many descendants as the stars and grains of sand on the seashore. Moreover these "offspring" will be victorious over their enemies and be a blessing to all the nations of the earth—all this "because you have **obeyed** My command" (22:15-18). From this first mention we learn that obedience means that a person must trust Yahweh so completely that whatever He requires must be done—no questions asked!

And this truth brings up a problem. Who among us is able to be consistently obedient? Surely Yahweh doesn't expect us sinners—with all our natural weaknesses and tendencies toward disobedience to be like Abraham—all the time! Here is precisely where a Name makes the difference—the difference between our poverty and His provision. *Yahweh Yireh* means **"I AM the One who provides whatever you need in order to be all that I require you to be."** In the story of Abraham and Isaac, we find Yahweh providing more than a ram to take Isaac's place and prevent Abraham from slaying his son. He also provided everything Abraham needed to obey Him. He supplied the basis for Abraham's faith by fulfilling all His promises. He gave this man the ability to trust and obey. Sure, Abraham was free to doubt Yahweh; he could have refused to obey. But Yahweh made the difference through many past experiences where He had shown Himself trustworthy.

Past Provision

What does all this means to us today? God is described as being "the same yesterday, today, and forever" (Hebrews 13:8). Consider these three time frames: yesterday, today, and forever—past, present, and future. First, what difference has Yahweh Yireh made in **our past**? Each of us has a testimony at this point. We can relate to time after time when Yahweh has supplied all we needed. Our greatest spiritual need is salvation—to be delivered from the penalty and power of our sin. Can you tell of your own conversion experience—that time when you know you were born again and became an heir of the King?

I think of a man I know named Don Harmon. He and his wife Shirley are among the most faithful servants of our church. Whenever some work project is needed at the church, we can depend on the Harmons to be there. Every Sunday he is standing at the church door to greet me with a big smile and warm handshake. Just a few years ago, Don was completely given to this world and all its pleasures. His own testimony is, "I turned my back on God so often and so long that He didn't know what my face looked like!" But through the outreach ministry of our church he was led to repent of his sin, believe the gospel message, and be saved. What a difference Yahweh Yireh has made—the difference between Don's spiritual poverty and Yahweh's abundant provision.

Present Provision

What about **the present**? Several months ago, a physician told Don that he had cancer. Since that time Don has gone through chemotherapy treatments. A recent MRI revealed the bad news that the treatments were not helpful. Subsequently, Don had a bone marrow transplant, spending over 40 days in the hospital. The Harmons along with many of our church members have prayed earnestly for Don's healing. Where is Yahweh Yireh? Has he forsaken this couple? Is He not hearing our prayers?

Don's testimony is: "God is always faithful to us; His answer to our prayers is not always what we ask, but always what is best. If He chooses to heal me, fine; if not, that's still okay because I will just go to be with Him in a far better place. I don't worry about this; I haven't lost any sleep over it. I can truthfully say this cancer has been the best thing that ever happened to me because it awaked me to what is really important in life." What a remarkable affirmation of Yahweh Yireh—He provides whatever we need!

What is true for Don and Shirley is true for everyone. Every day Yahweh proves Himself faithful to His promises. Just as He said to Joshua, "I will be with you, just as I was with Moses. I will not leave you or forsake you" (Joshua 1:5). There will be times when we are not aware of His presence; we may even feel forsaken. However, we must live by faith, not by sight. As one friend said, "We must learn to doubt our doubts and trust His trustworthiness."

[Shortly before this book was published, Don was promoted to his heavenly home. Now Shirley is an outstanding example of Yahweh's provision for all the comfort and strength she needs.]

Future Provision

Now focus on **the future**. Several Bible passages come to mind that give assurance about God's preparation for us. These words comfort me: "What no eye has seen and no ear has heard, and what has never come into a man's heart, is what God has prepared for those who love Him" (Hebrews 2:9). The future is as bright as the promises of God! Regardless of present trials, we can be strongly optimistic about tomorrow and all the tomorrows after that.

One of my personal disciplines is to remain in bed a few minutes after awaking each morning and offer this prayer: "Dear Yahweh, thank You for a night of rest and renewed strength. On the altar of my bed, I present myself as a living sacrifice to you. Throughout this new day my times are in Your hands." This commitment comes from Paul's words, "Therefore, brothers, by the mercies of God, I urge you to present your bodies as a living sacrifice, holy and pleasing to God; this is your spiritual worship" (Romans 12:1), and the words of the psalmist: "But as for me, I trust in You, O Yahweh, I say, 'You are my God.' My times are in Your hand" (Psalm 31:14-15 NKJV).

Such an affirmation of surrender and trust opens the door for Yahweh's best provision for each day. As with Abraham, Yahweh may choose to give me a "test," but I can be certain that this is part of His plan for my best. As He said to His people in their exile in Babylon, "I know the plans I have for you"—this is Yahweh's declaration—"plans for your welfare, not for disaster, to give you a future and a hope" (Jeremiah 29:11).

Every day is a new adventure—a time of discovering more about Yahweh and, with His help, discovering more about ourselves. I am impressed with these words from John Stott:

> *Life is a pilgrimage of learning, a voyage of discovery, in which our mistaken views are corrected, our distorted notions adjusted, our shallow opinions deepened and some of our vast ignorances diminished. (Christian Mission in the Modern World, p. 10).*

Eternal Provision

The more distant future also is well covered in Yahweh's provision. Jesus gave true comfort to His troubled disciples when He promised, "Your heart must not be troubled. Believe in God; believe also in Me. In My Father's house are many dwelling places; if not, I would have told you. I am going away to prepare a place for you. If I go away and prepare a place for you, I will come back and receive you to Myself, so that where I am you may be also" (John 14:1-3). One Bible interpreter has stated, "God created this amazing and beautiful earth in seven days, can you imagine what has been prepared for us by Jesus in all the years since He left?"

The "Heroes of the Faith" chapter, Hebrews 11, makes this declaration concerning those early saints, "These all died in faith without having received the promises, but they saw them from a distance, greeted them, and confessed that they were foreigners and temporary residents on the earth . . . . Therefore, God is not ashamed to be called their God, for He has prepared a city for them" (Hebrews 11:13-16). Yes, our ultimate future destination as Yahweh's people is secure because of that preparation He has made for us—the new heaven and the new earth (Revelation 21:1).

A pastor once asked me, "Do you know which Bible verse is a summary of the entire message of the Bible?" I guessed, "John 3:16." "No," he replied, "the central message of the Bible is given in Philippians 4:19." Here it is: "My God will supply all your needs according to His riches in glory in Christ Jesus." That's it! **Yahweh Yireh—I AM the One who**

Yahweh Yireh—I AM the One who provides whatever you need to become all I want you to be and do.

23

provides whatever you need to become all I want you to be and do.
This Name makes the difference between our poverty and His provision.

My feeble hope in miracles had waned,
My faith that He would soon provide was strained,
Then, prompted by His Spirit, my heart cried,
Yahweh Yireh! My Savior will provide.

My needs were great but greater than my need
Was He—Yahweh Yireh, so quick to heed
And help, to hold, to hide me from the storm
And shelter through the darkest night till morn.

Charles U. Wagner

Suggested prayer: **Gracious Father, thank You for revealing Yourself as Yahweh Yireh, the One who continually supplies all we need. Forgive us when we forget that You have repeatedly proven Your faithfulness to all Your promises, especially the promise provide for us. Deliver us from anxious fears. Use us as witnesses of Your unfailing love and care. Amen**

STUDY GUIDE

Chapter Two: The Difference Between Our
Poverty and God's Provision

1. Consider the following areas of spiritual poverty. Number them in order of your sense of personal need.

   _____ A lack of understanding God and His ways
   _____ Fear of failure
   _____ A tendency to resort to your ways rather than God's way
   _____ An unwillingness to obey God
   _____ A reluctance to wait on God to fulfill His promises

2. Review Abraham's experience with God from Genesis 22:1-19. Respond to these questions:

   What was the purpose of God's testing of Abraham?

   What is the evidence that Abraham trusted God?

   How does the term Yahweh Yireh relate to Abraham's experience?

3. How does Abraham's understanding of *Yahweh Yireh* offer help in your areas of spiritual poverty?

CHAPTER THREE

The Difference Between Our Sickness and His Healing

YAHWEH ROPHE
(YAH-way RO-fay)

CHAPTER TWO HELPED US understand the meaning of Yahweh Yireh—I AM the One who provides whatever you need. Chapter Three begins a series of more combination names showing specific ways in which Yahweh supplies these needs. We find the first of these special terms in Exodus 15:22-26.

Yahweh Yireh performed amazing miracles in order to liberate His people from over 400 years of bondage in Egypt. The "icing on the cake" was the crossing of the Red Sea on dry ground, followed by the return of the waters to drown the pursuing Egyptian army. How impressed the Israelites must have been. These pilgrims were on their way to the Promised Land assured of the adequate provisions of Yahweh Yireh. Exodus 15 records the songs of Moses and his sister Miriam and all the Israelites as they celebrated God's deliverance. Notice these words affirming Yahweh's faithful provisions:

"Yahweh, who is like You among the gods? Who is like You, glorious in holiness, revered with praises, performing wonders? You stretched out Your right hand, and the earth swallowed them. You will lead the people You have redeemed with Your steadfast love; You will guide them to Your holy dwelling with Your strength" (Exodus 15:11-13).

However, the first challenge in this journey revealed how little the people had learned from all these miracles. After a three-day journey in the wilderness, the water supply was depleted. All they could find was undrinkable bitter water at a place they named Marah ("bitter"). So they "grumbled to Moses, 'What are we going to drink?'" (Exodus 15:24). Moses wisely called upon Yahweh for help. The Lord showed him a tree which Moses cast into the water to make it drinkable—another miracle!

This action was intended by Yahweh to be a **test** for Israel. His words to them were: "If you will carefully obey Yahweh your God, do what is right in His eyes, pay attention to His commands, and keep all His statutes, I will not inflict any illness on you I inflicted on the Egyptians. For I am Yahweh who heals you" (Exodus 15:26). These last words in Hebrew are ***Yahweh-Rophe*** which means, "**I AM the One who heals.**" Just as He healed the water of bitterness, He promised to provide whatever healing His people needed.

The Hebrew word "rophe" (or "rapha" or "rophecha") means "to restore," "to heal," or "make whole." Although this combination name occurs just one time, the same term for "healing" is found more than sixty times in the Old Testament. This work of restoration is applied to various areas of need, such as physical illnesses, broken relationships, spiritual maladies, and even the healing of nations. In other words, **Yahweh can restore wholeness wherever needed.**

Before moving beyond this first Scripture reference, notice these words: "Then they came to Elim, where there were 12 springs of water and 70 date palms, and they camped there by the waters" (Exodus 15:27). What a clear testimony to the way Yahweh not only meets the needs of His people, but does so with **abundance**—not just one but 12 springs of water, plus luscious date palms! One of my favorite expressions of this truth comes from Paul's letter to the Corinthians: "God is able to make every grace overflow to you, so that in every way, always having everything you need, you may excel in every good work" (2 Corinthians 9:8). My wife has a neat statement about this truth, printed on a pillow: "I am drinking from my saucer, 'cause my cup is running over!" This name **Yahweh-Rophe makes the difference between our sickness and His health; our want and His abundance!**

> *Yahweh-Rophe makes the difference between our sickness and His health; our want and His abundance!*

27

Yahweh's Healing for Our Physical Sicknesses

The focus now turns to various areas where Yahweh-Rophe makes a difference, beginning with our physical ailments. Consider the enormous way in which physical maladies affect us and our entire culture. Are you astounded? Just suppose everyone had perfect health; what a difference that would make in our lives. No physicians and other health care givers, no medical schools, no hospitals and other similar care facilities, no pharmacies, no medical research, no medical insurance would exit. Think of the impact this change would make on our entire life-style and culture!

God's plan in the beginning was for such a Garden of Eden existence. Adam and Eve enjoyed perfect health in a perfect environment—no harmful bacteria, no diseases, no sickness. What happened? Sin. All our physical maladies are the product of rebellion against God, of choosing to disobey Him. This fact does not mean that every illness we have is due to our personal disobedience to God. However, Jesus' disciples thought this way. Recall the incident of His healing of a man who was born blind. The disciples asked Jesus, "Rabbi, who sinned, this man or his parents, that he was born blind?" Jesus replied, "Neither this man nor his parents sinned [to cause this]" (John 9:1-3). However, all physical imperfections are the consequence of sin in the human family. Adam and Eve were complete and whole in every aspect prior to their decision to choose their way rather than God's.

The infinite love, mercy, and grace of Yahweh are seen in the way He deals with physical illnesses in humankind. *Yahweh Rophe* brings healing and restoration, according to His will and purpose. In the first place, God has created human bodies with an amazing capacity to overcome illnesses, accidents, and all kinds of harmful happenings. **None of us can even imagine how often our bodies have resisted and overcome diseases that could easily have resulted in death.** We have suffered cuts, bruises, broken bones, and yet recovered. All because of Yahweh Rohe.

Scripture also records numerous accounts when the normal healing process was caused to miraculously quicken so as to give instant restoration. Again, Yahweh Rophe was the miracle worker. The initial fame of Jesus was due to His work of healing many sick and afflicted people. We are given this picture of Him immediately following the choosing of His twelve apostles:

"After coming down with them, He stood on a level place with a large crowed of His disciples and a great multitude of people . . . came to hear Him and to be healed of their diseases; and those tormented by unclean spirits were made well. The whole crowd was trying to touch Him, because power was coming out from Him and healing them all" (Luke 6:17-19). What was the source of this amazing power to heal? Yahweh Rophe!

We have all known of miraculous healings. One of the most impressive for me occurred several years ago when my friend, Henry Ray, was having surgery at a local hospital for rotator cuff repair on his shoulder. About 45 minutes into this rather routine procedure, his heart stopped beating. The surgeon immediately began his attempt to restore a heart beat. A total of 16 electric shocks were given to Henry's lifeless heart—all to no avail. Despite 90 minutes of intense efforts, nothing worked. His heart monitor showed a flat line.

By this time the waiting room was filled with friends who were earnestly praying for a miracle. Henry's pastor had been called and brought several friends to be with Susanne, Henry's wife. Finally, the doctors gave up and nurses began removing IVs and surgical equipment. Suddenly, they heard a beep on the heart monitor, then another, and soon a strong indication that this man, given up for dead, was alive!

Susanne rushed to his side and through her tears welcomed Henry back to life after 90 minutes of death. The doctor warned her of possible damage to Henry's heart, brain, and other organs after that length of time without oxygen. However, this 55 year-old man suffered no adverse effects from this trauma. In fact, a heart specialist examined him later and said, "You have the heart of a 25 year-old man!" Now Henry speaks in many churches giving his testimony of God's healing. Yahweh Rophe!

Although these dramatic kinds of restoration are seldom known to most of us, they are occurring in many places every day. Such miracles should not come as a surprise to us. Listen to these biblical statements on this subject:

"He Himself bore our sicknesses, and He carried our pains . . . . He was pierced because of our transgressions, crushed because of our iniquities; punishment for our peace was on Him, and we are healed by His wounds" (Isaiah 53:4-5).

"Jesus sent out these 12 after giving them instructions: ' . . . heal the sick, raise the dead, cleanse those with skin diseases, drive out demons . . . .'" (Matthew 10:5, 8).

"My soul, praise the LORD, and all that is within me, praise His holy name . . . and do not forget all His benefits. He forgives all your sin; He heals all your diseases" (Psalm 103:1-3).

How do you respond to those times when we claim these promises and God does not seem to answer—at least like we expect Him to? Here is my personal testimony regarding this kind of concern. My dad died from lung cancer when he was only 59 years old. At this time I was a young pastor with limited experience in praying for those who are sick. During the months of his illness I led my small church to pray for his healing, firmly believing that God would answer our prayers. Early one morning I was standing by his bed in the Presbyterian Hospital in Albuquerque, New Mexico. He was in an oxygen tent when he began breathing slower and slower. I was holding his hand when he gradually stopped breathing. A nurse came and examined him, "Your father is gone," she said.

This loss was a real faith-crisis for me. What went wrong? We all prayed believing God's promises to hear and answer our prayers. His full recovery was sincerely expected. But he died. I was very disappointed and rather confused. Our family was comforted to know he was a Christian and was in heaven with his Savior. We were just not ready to give him up so soon.

Some days later, as I was praying and seeking to understand what happened. The Holy Spirit put this thought in my heart: Your prayers were answered; your dad was healed—permanently. Only then did I remember that **all physical healing is temporary; this body of ours will surely die some day.** Whatever physical restoration we experience will not last very long. The awareness of this truth gave me peace.

Such a way of thinking will seem like a cop-out to some persons. But for me this insight makes sense. Many are healed temporarily in response to the prayers of faith; this blessing is God's will for them. But others, like my dad, are called "home." And this deliverance is God's final, permanent healing—no more sickness, no more pain.

Since this learning experience, I have prayed many times for those who were seriously ill, claiming their healing in faith. And sometimes they have recovered and sometimes not. As pastor I continue to follow this biblical advice:

"Is anyone among you sick: He should call for the elders of the church, and they should pray over him after anointing him with olive oil in the name of the Lord. The prayer of faith will save the sick person, and the Lord will raise him up; and if he has committed sins, he will be forgiven" (James 5:13-15).

Regardless of the outcome of our prayers for physical healing, we must pray with the awareness that our will is not always best—not always God's perfect will. However, **all healings of this body, whether temporary or permanent, are the work of Yahweh Rophe.**

Yahweh's Healing of Our Spiritual Sicknesses

God has made us in His image and likeness. This work of creation means we are basically spiritual in nature—our physical "tent" is just temporary housing for the real person we are. Spiritual maladies that need Yahweh's healing touch exist for everyone. Sickness of soul and spirit also are just as real, and far more serious than any illness of this body.

Yahweh Rophe is the Great Physician of our spiritual sicknesses. Of course, our primary spiritual need because of our sin is to be resurrected from spiritual death. As the apostle Paul said, "And you were dead in your trespasses and sins in which you previously walked according to this worldly age . . . . But God who is abundant in mercy, because of His great love that He had for us, made us alive with the Messiah even though we were dead in trespasses" (Ephesians 2:1-5). All who trust Yeshua for salvation experience a "new birth,"—a resurrection from spiritual death. The new life we have is literally His life in us, again Paul wrote, "Christ lives in me" (Galatians 2:20). Talk about a miracle, **here is the miracle of miracles!!**

Think about the man who wrote these words. His pre-conversion name was Saul. We read in Acts of how devoted he was to the destruction of

Jesus' influence and teachings. He literally despised all followers of Jesus and believed his religious duty was to remove them from any contact with non-Christians. However, on his way to the city of Damascus, with letters in hand that would identify those whom he would seize and carry away to prison, he had a life-changing experience. The resurrected Jesus appeared to him personally and began the process of transforming this radical persecutor into a radical preacher of the very gospel he sought to destroy. What a miraculous spiritual healing!

Can you think of anyone today who needs this kind of restoration? Sometimes we are deceived into thinking that some individuals are beyond redemption, so we don't pray for them or seek to reach them. Allow me to challenge you at this point. Call upon Yahweh Rophe on behalf of this person. Ask for the miracle of a new birth—a new creation.

Think now about a different kind of spiritual sickness, the kind only saved people can have. One of the recurring themes of God's messages to His people through the Old Testament prophets was that of the unfaithfulness ("backsliding") of His people. Yahweh repeatedly called His wayward people to return to Him. Listen to this promise given through the prophet Jeremiah: "Return, you faithless children. I will heal your unfaithfulness (backsliding)" (Jeremiah 3:22). Here is an example of the spiritual healing needed by God's people. The same Hebrew word for "healing" (rophe) is used in this appeal as in previous biblical references.

Sometimes the same healing is needed today. Who of us has not departed from a faithful walk with Yahweh? The most devoted follower of Yeshua struggles with the issue of faithfulness. Each morning I read a hymn and the story of how it was written. Recently, the hymn was titled "He the Pearly Gates Will Open." The author was a Swedish man named Fredrick Arvid Blom. After moving to the United States in the 1890's, he became an officer in the Salvation Army. Later he was the pastor of several churches. Through a series of regrettable circumstances he fell into deep sin and was sent to prison. His testimony was, "I drifted from God…became embittered with myself, the world, and with fellow ministers who looked on me with suspicion." Later Blom returned to the Salvation Army and the pastorate.

Verses two and three of this hymn reflect his experience:

Like a sparrow hunted, frightened, weak and helpless—so was I;
Wounded, fallen, yet He healed me—He will heed the sinner's cry.

Love divine, so great and wondrous! All my sins He then forgave!
I will sing His praise forever, for His blood, His pow'r to save.

Chorus:
He the pearly gates will open, So that I may enter in; for He purchased my redemption
And forgave me all my sin.

Yahweh Rophe is the only One who can bring spiritual healing and restoration to sinners.

At times each of us needs to pray with the psalmist: "I said, 'Yahweh, be gracious to me; **heal** me, for I have sinned against You'" (Psalm 41:4).

Yahweh's Healing of Our Emotional Needs

God has given us many emotions, such as joy and sorrow, love and hate, peace and distress, courage and fear. Each of these feelings has the potential of being a blessing or a problem, depending on the situation where they are expressed. Some persons experience emotional illnesses when such feelings get out of control. The Bible speaks of a condition called brokenheartedness. Such grief may arise from the loss of some one or some thing of great value. One expression of this sorrow is disappointment in ourselves, others, or even God.

Isaiah spoke of the Messiah making this claim for Himself: "The Spirit of the Lord God is on Me, because Yahweh has anointed Me to bring good news to the poor. He has sent me to **heal the brokenhearted**, to proclaim liberty to the captives, and freedom to the prisoners; to proclaim the year of Yahweh's favor…." (Isaiah 61:1-2). Then Luke records an occasion as Jesus began His public ministry by going to His home synagogue in Nazareth. He stood up and read this same passage from Isaiah. When he finished He said, "Today as you listen, the Scripture has been fulfilled" (Luke 4:21).

The work of healing the brokenhearted is continued today in the ministry of **Yahweh Rophe**. Just as the psalmist declared, "Yahweh…

heals the brokenhearted and binds up their wounds" (Psalm 147:3). One example is: A single mom and her two small daughters were about to be evicted from their house. Her job did not provide enough income to meet all their expenses. She, along with several Christian friends, was claiming God's provision for this need. Finally, with a broken heart, she appeared in court and received the bad news of foreclosure. As she was leaving the courthouse, a man approached her and said, "I was in the court and heard your story; I may be able to help you." This stranger helped her get in touch with a woman from a local church who made arrangements whereby this mother kept her house. Following this blessing, she told a friend that on the way to the court she was praying for God's help. Her car radio was tuned to a Christian station and she heard these words from a song: "God is here! Let the brokenhearted rejoice."

Perhaps you or someone you know is suffering from some form of emotional brokenness. The wise course of action is to call on Yahweh Rophe and claim His healing. Too often when we are hurting we turn to others first, rather than to the Great Physician. An interesting example of this mistake is found in the actions of a man named Asa, the king of Judah. Notice this text: "In the thirty-ninth year of his reign, Asa developed a disease in his feet, and his disease became increasingly severe. Yet even in his disease he didn't seek Yahweh but the physicians. Asa died in the forty-first year of his reign and rested with his fathers" (2 Chronicles 16:12).

This ruler relied upon physicians for two years rather than Yahweh Rophe. Unfortunately, these men were not able to help him. His condition worsened until he died. This episode does not mean that we should not seek the best medical help we can find. However, our ultimate trust should be in the Great Physician to work His healing through physicians and their treatments. Remember that all healing comes from Yahweh. He makes the difference between our sickness and His healing.

Yahweh's Healing of Our Broken Relationships

The media presents news about well known leaders in the fields of politics, sports, and religion who have suffered broken marriages due to some form of infidelity. Unfortunately most of these situations end as a permanent broken relationship—a divorce. Recently, a couple, whose marriage was threatened by the husband's affair, appeared on several TV talk shows because their marriage had been saved. The difference was clear. The offended wife agreed to forgive her unfaithful husband. When she was questioned by the host of the show, she simply said, "I must forgive him because the Lord has often forgiven me."

Many broken relationship can be mended by forgiveness, if the offender is willing to admit his or her wrong doing. Every Christian has experienced the healing of the most important of all broken relationships—our separation from God. How amazing is His forgiveness, especially in light of our utter unworthiness of such favor. Yahweh's promises to forgive are numerous and each one is a wonder of love, mercy, and grace. Consider these encouraging words:

"If My people who are called by My name humble themselves, pray and seek My face, and turn from their evil ways, then I will hear from heaven, forgive their sin, and heal their land" (2 Chronicles 7:14).

"In Him we have redemption through His blood, the forgiveness of our trespasses, according to the riches of His grace that He lavished on us with all wisdom and understanding" (Ephesians 1:7-8).

"If we confess our sins, He is faithful and righteous to forgive us our sins and to cleanse us from all unrighteousness" (1 John 1:9).

"Look, the days are coming...when I will make a new covenant . . . . I will place My law within them and write it on their hearts. I will be their God, and they will be My people . . . I will forgive their wrongdoing and never again remember their sin" (Jeremiah 31:31-34).

"You have thrown all my sins behind Your back" (Isaiah 38:17).

"He will vanquish our iniquities. You will cast all our sins into the depths of the sea" (Micah 7:19).

One teacher summarized the truths of these last three scriptures by stating: "God says He will forgive our sins, cast them behind His back in the depths of the sea, and remember them no more. Then He puts up a sign there saying, NO FISHING!" In other words, we must learn to accept God's forgiveness and forgive ourselves.

Perhaps the most difficult personal action is forgiving someone who has intentionally wronged us. Our emotions get in the way; we feel resentment toward that person, even wanting revenge. But **forgiveness is not an option. We who have been forgiven by Yahweh must forgive others.** Our Lord said, "If you forgive people their wrongdoing, your heavenly Father will forgive you as well. But if you don't forgive people, your Father will not forgive your wrongdoing" (Matthew 6:14-15).

This necessity of forgiving others is repeated several times in Matthew, Mark, and Luke. Then Paul gave this command: "Therefore, God's chosen ones, holy and loved, put on heartfelt compassion, kindness, humility, gentleness, and patience, accepting one another and forgiving one another if anyone has a complaint against another. Just as the Lord has forgiven you, so also you must forgive" (Colossians 3:12-13).

What does forgiving someone involve? What does this essential action mean? I've heard friends say, "I can forgive but I can't forget; so, I guess I haven't forgiven." There is a difference between forgiving and forgetting. Painful experiences may never be forgotten, but to forgive means to choose not to hold a grudge against someone who has wronged us. We decide to let go of any claim for revenge, refusing to let the offense become a barrier between us and them. We never again remind the offender of the offense—it's over. The hurt may be remembered but the hate is gone.

How can this happen? First, admit that such mercy comes only from Yahweh Rophe. He alone can enable us to express His forgiveness to others. Recall Moses' experience of casting a tree in the water at Marah to miraculously remove the bitterness. Yahweh could have shown him a stone or some dirt to cast in the water, but He chose a tree. Why? I believe that tree pointed to the death of the Messiah on a tree (cross) centuries later. That event would permanently remove the bitterness of our sinful shame and guilt before God.

Unforgiveness is a form of bitterness. And bitterness will poison our spirit, causing much unnecessary torment. Forgiving others not only blesses them but also us. We are set free from the emotionally harmful effects of that resentment. You may recall the beautiful biblical story of Naomi recorded in the book of Ruth. This woman suffered the loss of her husband and her two sons in a foreign country. When she returned to her homeland as a widow, she said to those who welcomed her, "Don't call me Naomi ("pleasant"). Call me Mara ("bitter"), for the Almighty has made me very bitter. I left full, but Yahweh has brought me back empty. Why do you call me Naomi, since Yahweh has pronounced judgment on me, and the Almighty has afflicted me?" (Ruth 1:20-21).

The narrative continues to tell the story of God's providence in providing a husband for Ruth, Naomi's daughter-in-law. Later a son is born to Ruth and Boaz. He was Obed, who became the grandfather of David. Naomi had blamed God for her losses. Now she was delivered from her bitterness through the blessings of Yahweh Rophe. Likewise, the same Healer is continually working to change our disappointments into His appointments.

Jeremiah now becomes our example. He is often referred to as the "Weeping Prophet" because of his sorrow over the sinful condition of God's chosen people. One of his laments has these sad words: "My joy has flown away; grief has settled on me. My heart is sick. Listen—the cry of my dear people from a far away land: Is Yahweh no longer in Zion, her King not in her midst? Why have they provoked Me to anger with their graven images, with their worthless foreign idols: Harvest has passed, summer has ended, but we have not been saved. I am broken by the brokenness of my dear people. I mourn; horror has taken hold of me. Is there no balm in Gilead: Is there no physician there? So why has the healing of my dear people not come about?"(Jeremiah 8:18-22).

Gilead was a region near Judah where the storax tree produced a balm (resin) that was used medicinally. Jeremiah used this well known medication as an example of how Yahweh's healing of their sin sickness was available but was not being applied. An old Afro-American spiritual song refers to this same illustration:

Sometimes I feel discouraged and think my work's in vain,
But then the Holy Spirit revives my soul again.

If you cannot preach like Peter, if you cannot pray like Paul,
You can tell the love of Jesus, and say, "He died for all."

Chorus:
There is a balm in Gilead to make the wounded whole,
There is a balm in Gilead to heal the sin-sick soul.

Yes, a healing balm is available whatever your problem may be. That effective remedy is **Yahweh Rophe**. If we trust Him and wait patiently upon Him, He will be the difference between our sickness and His healing.

Yahweh's Healing of All Things

Yahweh's ultimate work of restoration and healing will be revealed when He brings an end to this present world and all its imperfections. The last chapter of the Old Testament gives a glimpse of this cataclysmic event. The prophet Malachi was inspired to record this message of Yahweh: "For indeed, the day is coming, burning like a furnace, when all the arrogant and everyone who commits wickedness will become stubble. The coming day will consume them, says Yahweh Sabaoth, not leaving them root or branches. But for you who fear My name, the sun of righteousness will rise with healing in its wings, and you will go out and playfully jump like calves from the stall. You will trample the wicked, for they will be ashes under the soles of your feet on the day I am preparing, says Yahweh Sabaoth" (Malachi 4:1-3).

Likewise, the final chapters of the New Testament echo this promise of ultimate restoration. The apostle John described his vision regarding the future in these amazing words: "Then I saw a new heaven and a new earth, for the first heaven and the first earth had passed away.... Then the One seated on the throne said, 'Look! I am making everything new...'" (Revelation 21:1-5). Eventually, God will completely restore this world to its original state of perfection—like the Garden of Eden in the beginning.

The final vision of the Bible gives a brief description of this renewed paradise. John said of the angel who revealed it to him, "Then he showed me the river of living water, sparkling like crystal, flowing from the throne of God and of the Lamb down the middle of the broad street of the city. On both sides of the river was the tree of life bearing 12 kinds of fruit, producing its fruit every month. The leaves of the tree are for healing the nations, and there will no longer be any curse" (Rev. 22:1-3). How interesting that here is another tree for healing—just like the one at Marah. Only the leaves of this tree bring complete healing and restoration to all the nations—all those who are in heaven. There will be no more sin, nor results of sin, no more curse—all things are new; all are perfect. **All praise be to Yahweh Rophe!**

Suggested prayer: **Gracious Great Physician, we are humbled by a new awareness of Your love for us and Your power to make a difference in us. Forgive us for failing so often to look to You for all our healing needs. We thank you for the skill and resources you give to physicians and counselors, but we know that all kinds of restoration ultimately come from You.**

Thank You, Yahweh Rophe, for working continually for our wholeness. Make us more keenly aware of the miracles of healing You perform every day. Teach us to acknowledge Your ability to deliver us from all our sicknesses. We praise You and we worship You as our only hope of complete and final healing. Amen

STUDY GUIDE

Chapter Three: The Difference Between
Our Sickness and His Healing

1. List the five areas of life-needs where Yahweh Rophe makes a difference.

    a.

    b.

    c.

    d.

    e.

2. Read the following Scripture passages that express various areas of Yahweh Rophe's healing and restoration. Match the correct answers with a straight line from the second column to the Scripture passage.

    Ephesians 2:1-5   Emotional needs

    James 5:13-15   Broken relationships

    Revelation 22:1-3   Spiritual Sickness

    Ephesians 1:7-8   Healing all things

    Isaiah 61:1-2   Physical sickness

3. Briefly describe an area in your life where you felt your need for Yahweh Rophe. How can you appropriate His provision for this need?

CHAPTER FOUR

The Difference Between Our Defeat and His Victory

YAHWEH NISSI
(YAH-way NIS-see)

I SAW A MAN with these sad words tattooed on his arm: "Born to Lose." He chose that message because his life had been one of continual defeat. He had been overcome by various temptations, such as stealing, drug use, and various crimes that placed him in prison. Thus he saw himself as a born loser.

The book market today is flooded with self-help volumes on how to be a successful person. Many religious leaders give their followers the message that the secret to happiness and a life of fulfillment lies within them. They claim that the best way to become what we should be and want to be is to think positively, try harder, and have faith in oneself.

If we take the Bible seriously and subscribe to its authority, we conclude that we are all born to lose. None of us has the natural ability to make ourselves become successful in the truest sense of that word. The psalmist accurately described every person in these plaintive words: "The wicked go astray from the womb; liars err from birth" (Psalm 58:3).

All people are born with a nature that is flawed, one that will always choose to rebel against God. The apostle Paul had more to say about this old nature, which he called the "flesh" than any other writer of biblical truth. He said, "I know that nothing good lives in me, that is, in my flesh. For the desire to do what is good is with me, but there is no ability to do it . . . . I discover this principle: when I want to do good, evil

41

is with me. For in my inner self I joyfully agree with God's law. But I see a different law in the parts of my body, waging war against the law of my mind and taking me prisoner to the law of sin in the part of my body" (Romans 7:18-23).

However, good news has been given! The good news for us sinners, continually being defeated by our old sinful nature, is that we can have a new nature, a nature that is turned toward God, not away from Him. This new nature begins with a new birth—a spiritual birth. **Our greatest need is not just to become nice but to become new.** This new nature which only God can give us is one of victory rather than defeat. Paul continued his words to say to the Romans, "What a wretched man I am! Who will rescue me from this body of death? I thank God through Jesus Christ our Lord!" (Romans 7:24-25).

Focus on another combination name of Yahweh that reveals this important truth. The historical setting is found in Exodus 17. Moses had led the people into the wilderness on their way to the Promised Land. When they came to a place named Rephidim, a people group called Amalekites confronted them. These residents refused to allow the Israelites to pass peaceably through their territory. In order to defend themselves, they attacked Israel. We now read of Israel's first warfare on this journey to God's appointed home.

Moses called upon a man named Joshua to choose warriors and form an army to defend themselves against the Amalekites. This is the first mention of Joshua who later became Moses' successor as leader of God's chosen people. Notice their strategy. Moses said that he, along with Aaron and Hur, would stand on top of a nearby hill to watch the battle and Moses would hold "God's staff" in his hand. As long as Moses was able to keep the staff uplifted, Israel prevailed in the battle, but when he tired and lowered his hands, the enemy prevailed.

Aaron and Hur came to his aid. These men had Moses sit on a large stone while they stood on either side holding up the rod in his hands till the sun went down and the battle was won. Yahweh told Moses to record this incident on a scroll as a reminder of what happened that day. The text reads: "And Moses built an altar and named it, 'The LORD Is My Banner' " (Exodus 17:15). **The Hebrew words for "The LORD Is My Banner" are *Yahweh nissi*.** The term *nissi* also may be translated "ensign" or "standard" or "my miracle." This word usually refers to any kind of visual symbol like a modern military flag to identify the soldier's object of loyalty.

Earlier in Exodus Moses' staff had been used as a symbol of God's authority and power when He parted the Red Sea (Exodus 14:15-22). Just prior to the battle with the Amalekites Moses was commanded to use the same rod to strike a huge rock to make water come forth (Exodus 17:5-6). This rod (staff) was a visible reminder of the miracles Yahweh performed for His people. Whenever Moses lifted the staff, the people knew victory was at hand.

Moses needed help to uphold the staff. This occasion reminds me of a similar happening during a Civil War battle at Thompson's Station, Tennessee. My wife and I learned of this interesting happening when we visited the home of our friends, Jay and Marcia Franks. Several years ago the Franks purchased this pre-Civil War house called Homestead Manor, built between 1809 and 1819. During our visit we were led down some narrow stairs to the cellar where a small window looks out toward the front yard.

We were told that during the Battle of Thompson's Station on March 5, 1863, several women and children took refuge in this small cellar. As the soldiers were fighting, these observers saw the color bearer of the 3rd Arkansas Regiment fall, having been shot by the enemy. Immediately, Alice Thompson, the 17 year-old daughter of the owners of the house, left the safety of the cellar, ran onto the battlefield and lifted the fallen regiment flag. The Confederate soldiers were so inspired by her courage that they went on to win the battle that day!

Visual symbols represent truths that can be very inspirational. Remember how you were moved to tears as the "Stars and Stripes" were displayed on special occasions? Military forces usually have some kind of flag or banner to remind them of the importance of their cause. Such an emblem can become a rallying point during times of danger.

I recently read this story of the writing of an old hymn text titled, "The Banner of the Cross." The author was Major Daniel Webster Whittle who was a soldier in the Civil War. After the war he was influenced by Dwight L. Moody to become an evangelist and hymn writer. Here's the text of one of his best known hymns written in 1877:

There's a royal banner given for display to the soldiers of the King;
As an ensign fair we lift it up today, while as ransomed ones we sing.
Though the foe may rage and gather as the flood, let the standard be displayed;
And beneath its folds, as soldiers of the Lord, for the truth be not dismayed!

Over land and sea, wherever man may dwell, make the glorious tidings known;
Of the crimson banner now the story tell, while the Lord shall claim His own!
When the glory dawns--'tis drawing very near—it is hastening day by day;
Then before our King the foe shall disappear and the cross the world shall sway!

Chorus:
Marching on, marching on. For Christ count everything but loss!
And to crown Him King, we'll toil and sing beneath the banner of the cross!

The inspiration for these words came from Psalm 60:4-12, "You have given a signal flag to those who fear You, so that they can flee before the archers….Give us aid against the foe, for human help is worthless. With God we will perform valiantly; He will trample our foes."

Major Whittle identified the Christian soldier's "signal flag" as being the cross. The cross reminds us of our source of victory over our enemies. I remember as a child marching into the church building for Vacation Bible School. Two flags were carried ahead of us by fellow students; one flag was the banner of the USA, the second was the Christian flag with the symbol of the cross. Upon arriving inside and standing at our seats, the pledge to each flag was recited.

Now, let's return to Moses and the Amalekites. Just as the Israelites were on their journey to God's promised destination, we also are pilgrims on a journey through life. And, like they faced enemies who engaged them in warfare, so do we. **The Christian life is never easy, never without**

opposition, never beyond attack from those who seek to destroy us.
This truth means we need to be on guard and to have a battle strategy in place. For the remainder of this chapter we will focus on three aspects of this continual battle: (1) the enemies, (2) the armor and weapons, and (3) the way to overcome.

Yahweh's Victory Over Our Enemies

"Green Day" is an American Rock trio formed in 1987. Although I am not a fan of their music, I want to borrow a thought from one of their songs, "Know Your Enemy." The opening lyrics are: "Do you know the enemy? Do you know your enemy? Well, gotta know the enemy." Those words remind me of a book written by Walt Kelly entitled: *Pogo: We have met the enemy and he is us!*

Every military leader will agree that one of **the first essentials in waging successful warfare is to identify the enemy.** Unfortunately, our enemies in the Christian warfare are very good at concealing themselves. As a result, many believers expend their efforts against the wrong adversary. For example have you known someone—perhaps yourself—who became involved with another person in some kind of conflict over hurt feelings or perhaps a quarrel resulting from a disagreement? The two parties spoke strongly against one another and a physical altercation occurred. Rather than engaging the actual enemy, these individuals or groups fell into Satan's trap. They assumed the other person was their foe. Wrong!

Discovering our true enemy comes from the revelation of God's Word, the Bible. The psalmist declared, "The revelation of Your words brings light and gives understanding to the inexperienced" (Psalm. 119:130). Our true adversary is never visible. His realm is one of darkness. The only way a person ever identifies this foe is by the shining light of God's Word. Apart from the Bible we would never know our enemy, and never understand his tactics.

Fortunately, the apostle Paul gives us much help at this point. He knew the adversary very well and shares valuable information with us. Perhaps the single most helpful biblical passage regarding spiritual warfare is found in Ephesians 6. Notice this exposure of our enemies: "For our battle is not against flesh and blood, but against the rulers, against the authorities, against the world powers of this darkness, against the spiritual forces of evil in the heavens" (Ephesians 6:12-14). These terms: "rulers," "authorities," "world powers of this darkness," "spiritual forces of evil in the heavens," all refer to Satan and his demons. These are opposed to Yahweh, His people, and all that is good. Notice the references to power and authority and forces. These enemies are formidable; they are capable of bringing great destruction.

Remember this truth: **People are not our enemies when it comes to spiritual warfare.** If we fight against other people, we will never defeat the real adversary. Never wage war, whether in words or actions, against another individual or group. Please understand, I am not referring to defending yourself if some person seeks to harm you, such as some form of physical abuse. Of course we fight back in those kinds of situations. But if someone speaks wrongfully to you or about you, remember that Satan, the real foe, is using them.

> *People are not our enemies when it comes to spiritual warfare.*

Victory over Satan. Only the Bible reveals the truth about Satan. He is called Lucifer, Beelzebub, the prince of the air, a roaring lion, a sower of tares, a wolf, a serpent, the accuser of the brethren, a devourer, and a liar. Moreover he is exposed as the devil, the prince of this world, the adversary, a dragon, the spirit that works in the children of disobedience, the father of lies, the tempter. All these terms speak of the various ways he seeks to attack us, deceive us, and defeat God's purpose for us.

On one occasion Jesus was warning about Satan's power. He compared him and his demons to thieves and robbers who stole sheep from the shepherd. Jesus described Satan's purpose, just like these evil persons, as those who came to "steal and to kill and to destroy" (John 10:10). We can make that application to Satan's design for each of us. He seeks to steal our joy, kill our effectiveness, and destroy our fellowship with Jesus. For this reason we must be diligent and continuously on guard.

Peter knew much about Satan from personal experience. Notice what he said in one of his letters about this enemy: "Be sober! Be on the alert! Your adversary the Devil is prowling around like a roaring lion, looking for anyone he can devour. Resist him, firm in the faith, knowing that the same sufferings are being experienced by your brothers in the world" (1 Peter 5:8-9). You are probably acquainted with fellow believers whose joy and usefulness for serving Christ has been devoured by this adversary. **Never assume that you are immune.**

Victory over the world. One writer compares the Holy Trinity (God the Father, Son, and Holy Spirit) to the unholy trinity (Satan, the world, and the flesh). The Holy Trinity is on our side; the unholy trinity is against us. Let's examine this unholy trinity. We have focused on Satan, now think about the world. When the Bible speaks of the world, several meanings are possible. The world of nature, the world of people, and the world where Satan is in control are all included. This last world is the one we need help in understanding how it relates to spiritual warfare. A good description of this particular world is: "The organized Satanic system that is opposed to God and hostile to Jesus and His followers. The non-Christian culture including governments, educational systems, and businesses." In other words, the term "world" sometimes is used in the Bible to refer to everything around us that is opposed to God, whether that be ungodly systems of education, entertainment, political agendas, religions, literature, governments, philosophies, non Christian people and so on. Satan controls this world. He uses this venue to oppose God and His people.

Jesus described Satan as "the ruler of this world" (John 12:31). Paul spoke of "this present evil age" (Galatians 1:4). John warned believers, "Do not love the world or the things that belong to the world. If anyone loves the world, love for the Father is not in him. Because everything that belongs to the world—the lust of the flesh, the lust of the eyes, and the pride in one's lifestyle—is not from the Father, but is from the world. And the world with its lust is passing away, but the one who does God's will remains forever" (1 John 2:15-17).

John 17 records the longest prayer of Jesus in the Bible. He makes several references to "the world" that are helpful. Notice these words: "I am not praying for the world but for those You have given Me . . . they are in the world . . . . The world hated them because they are not of the world . . . . I have sent them into the world . . . so that the world may believe You sent Me" (John 17:9-21). Jesus was asking that His followers who are in the world would not become like the world, but be His witnesses to the world.

Later, the apostle Paul called for believers not to be conformed to this world (Romans 12:2). One translation renders this command as: "Do not let the world squeeze you into its own mold." He declared that he considered himself dead to the world and the world dead to him (Galatians 6:14). James stated that friendship with the world was "hostility toward God" (James 4:4). These verses are warnings to us. Be diligently on guard against being unduly influenced by this world in which we live.

Therefore the challenge we face is that of continuing to live in a world system that is hostile toward God, controlled by Satan, and puts pressure on us to conform to its ungodly ways. How can we overcome such subtle and powerful influences? Again, we are indebted to the Word for an answer. John expressed the truth this way: ". . . whatever has been born of God conquers the world. This is the victory that has conquered the world: our faith. And who is the one who conquers the world but the one who believes that Jesus is the Son of God?" (1 John 5: 4-5). Just as surely as Jesus lived in the world but successfully resisted the world's pressures and ultimately overcame the world—so can we! Because we our faith connects us to Him, **His victory becomes our victory**.

A recent incident illustrates this victory. An Iranian Christian woman boarded a bus in Tehran to visit relatives outside the city. She carried copies of Bibles and the *JESUS* film in her travel bag. She knew that what she was doing was illegal in that country and she was risking her life. Her prayer that morning was that God would use her as His witness, protecting her from Islamic persecution. As she traveled on the bus, a movie was being shown on the monitor for all the riders to view. When the movie malfunctioned, she handed the *JESUS* film to the driver who inserted it into the video player. The forty passengers viewed the entire film as they journeyed together. When the movie ended, eight of them told this woman they were interested in becoming Christians, including the driver. Later she visited the driver and his family in their home. He, his wife, their three grown children, and his sister all prayed to receive Jesus as their Savior and Lord! **Yahweh Nissi! He who is our victory makes the difference between conforming to the world and the transforming of the world.**

Victory over the flesh. The Bible uses the term *flesh* in two ways. Sometimes the word refers to our physical body, such as "flesh and blood cannot inherit the kingdom of heaven." Other references use "flesh" to refer to our fallen human nature—that aspect of us that rebels against God. Paul says more about this kind of flesh than any other biblical writer. For example, the eighth chapter of Romans contains statements such as, "For the mind-set of the flesh is hostile to God because it does not submit itself to God's law, for it is unable to do so. Those whose lives are in the flesh are unable to please God" (vv.7-8).

All Christians have a new, second nature which is the Holy Spirit who lives in us. These two natures are in conflict—one against the other. Paul gives this wise counsel regarding this internal warfare: "I say then, walk by the Sprit and you will not carry out the desire of the flesh. For the flesh desires what is against the Spirit, and the Spirit desires what is against the flesh, these are opposed to each other" (Galatians 5:16-17). To "walk by the Spirit" means to proceed through each day with a deliberate dependence upon the Holy Spirit for victory over the old nature.

How can we identify which nature is in control? Paul describes the "works of the flesh" in these terms: "Sexual immorality, moral impurity, promiscuity, idolatry, sorcery, hatreds, strife, jealousy, outbursts of anger, selfish ambitions, dissensions, factions, envy, drunkenness, carousing, and anything similar" (Galatians 5:19-21). What a display of Satan-like characteristics! On the other hand the "fruit of the Spirit" is listed as "love, joy, peace, patience, kindness, goodness, faith, gentleness, self-control" (Galatians 5:22-23). On personal examination we can easily see whether the flesh or the Spirit is in control.

One writer describes the flesh as Satan's personal representative in us. Satan appeals to this old nature and seeks to work his evil schemes there. What can we do to overcome the flesh? Paul answered the question in these words: "Let us discard the deeds of darkness and put on the armor of light. Let us walk with decency, as in the daylight: not in carousing and drunkenness; not in sexual impurity and promiscuity, not in quarreling and jealousy. But put on the Lord Jesus Christ, and make no plans to satisfy the fleshly desires" (Romans 13:12-14).

And just what is this "armor of light"?

The Armor and Weapons Yahweh Nissi Gives for the Warfare

You noticed in the passage from Ephesians 6 that several parts of armor are listed. Paul wrote these words when he was a prisoner, closely guarded by Roman soldiers. As he looked at their armor he chose to compare that to the Christian's battle gear. Lets examine each piece of this armor to learn how we can best do battle with our adversaries in the spiritual warfare.

Truth like a belt around your waist (Ephesians 6:14a). A Roman soldier's wide belt was the most important part of his armor because it held his clothing and various items of his armor in place. If our warfare with the enemy is to be effective, we must begin and continue with truth. Remember the father of lies begins his attack with lies. Our first introduction to Satan is in the Garden of Eden. Among the first words he spoke to Eve was this lie, "No! You will not die [if you eat the forbidden fruit]" (Genesis 3:4). Jesus exposed this fact about Satan when He said, ". . . there is no truth in him. When he tells a lie, he speaks from his own nature, because he is a liar and the father of liars" (John 8:44).

Whatever comes to us that is false, has its origin with the devil (a word meaning "slanderer"). Truth is our defensive armor as well as our offensive weapon. We must always be on guard against speaking or behaving in ways that are contrary to truth. Our best resource is the Holy Spirit who is described as "the Spirit of truth." Among Jesus' final words to His disciples were these: "When the Spirit of truth comes, He will guide you into all the truth" (John 16:13).

The best way to know truth is by opening the Bible daily and claiming the teaching ministry of the Holy Spirit. Again, consider these words of Jesus to His followers, "If you continue in My word, you really are My disciples. You will know the truth, and the truth will set you free" (John 8:32).

Do you have the personal discipline of daily Bible reading? Perhaps my own practice can help you. I begin each day with a time of Bible reading and prayer. Using plastic tabs to mark the places in the Bible where I am reading, my progress through various chapters and books is easy to track. Each day's reading (perhaps a few verses) comes from the major portions of the Bible. Right now I am reading from the Pentateuch (first five books of the Old Testament), the Psalms, the prophets, the gospels, Acts, the New

Testament letters, and the Revelation. This practice may sound like more than you have time for, however, I can complete this reading in 15 minutes. My reading always begins with this simple prayer: "Yahweh, please open Your Word to my heart and open my heart to Your truth." Just the act of opening the Bible reminds me to pray this prayer for His opening of my heart and mind.

At other times I have chosen the discipline of following a schedule of reading the Bible through in a year—such as two chapters from the Old Testament and one from the New Testament each day (plus five chapters on Sunday). Let me encourage you to choose a plan that works for you. **The main thing is to be *in* His word every day so that His word can be *in* you.** This practice is the way to put on the belt of truth.

Righteousness like armor on your chest (6:14b). The Roman soldier needed this piece of armor to protect his heart and other vital organs from the enemy's attack. **We all need two kinds of righteousness; both are provided by Yahweh.** (In Chapter 7 we will learn more about this.) We need positional righteousness, which means to be declared righteous by Yahweh. We also need practical righteousness which means to behave in a right manner.

Satan is described as being the accuser (Revelation 12:10). He repeatedly accuses a believer of being unrighteous, both in our relationship with God and with others. In other words, he reminds us of our sins. When he attacks with these accusations, we must repel these "flaming arrows" with the truth that we have been declared righteous by Yahweh and forgiven all our unrighteousness in the past and we are being made righteous in our behavior in the present.

Feet sandaled with readiness for the gospel of peace (6:15). Paul begins this armor passage with references to standing against the tactics of the Devil (v. 11) and "take your stand. Stand, therefore" (vv. 13-14). In order to stand securely in this spiritual battle good footing is required. The soldier of that day wore thick-soled sandals, strapped to his feet, so he could keep from falling during hand-to-hand combat.

Our sure footing in spiritual warfare is the good news (gospel) of peace with Yahweh by means of His grace. Jesus declared this good news when He said, "Peace I leave with you. My peace I give to you" (John 14:27). By faith we possess this peace—the result of a righteous standing before

God. This fact is the firm foundation of our relationship with Him. Satan's attack can never overthrow us as long as we stand on this fact.

But notice Paul's wording again: "your feet sandaled with readiness for the gospel of peace." This translation reads a little differently from most. The Living Bible renders this verse as: "Wear shoes that are able to speed you on as you preach the Good News of peace with God." Our role as witnesses may often find us engaging the enemy as we are seeking to share this good news with others. Paul may be referring here to these words from Isaiah, "How beautiful on the mountains are the feet of the herald, who proclaims peace, who brings news of good things, who proclaims salvation, who says to Zion, 'Your God reigns!'" (Isaiah 52:7). At all times and in all places we must be ready to share an effective witness regarding the only way to peace with God.

In every situation take the shield of faith, with it you will be able to extinguish the flaming arrows of the evil one (v. 16). A soldier's shield was a rather large, two feet wide by four feet long, leather covered piece of solid wood. When "flaming arrows" were shot by the enemy, the soldier could stoop down behind this shield for protection.

These arrows were often dipped in a tar-like substance, set ablaze, and shot at the enemy. Paul compares these arrows to the various ways Satan attacks us. Examples would be the temptation to doubt our salvation or to question God's forgiveness of our sins or such temptations as lustful thoughts and desires, feelings of envy, jealousy, pride and other things that displease God. How do we cope with such thoughts?

Faith brings victory. But how do we get this kind of faith? Paul answers our question in this way, "So faith comes from what is heard, and what is heard comes through the message about Christ" (Romans10:17). Faith is not some wishful hope or a strong desire or positive thinking. **Faith is a confident expectation based on truth—the truth we hear from God's Word about His faithfulness to all He promises.** Thus we must choose to exercise trust in the promises of God. For example, when tempted to doubt if God has forgiven your sins, claim His promise to forgive. Actually quote these words: "If we confess our sins, He is faithful and righteous to forgive us our sins and to cleanse us from all unrighteousness" (1 John 1:9). Then thank God for His faithfulness to this promise. This is the shield of faith.

Preparation is needed for other similar attacks from the enemy. He knows our weakness. Perhaps you worry. You find yourself having personal feelings of anxiety about your health, your financial security, your family or other similar matters. Ask God to show you a Bible promise that meets this need, memorize it, and affirm this promise by faith every time the temptation occurs. When I first sensed that God was calling me to be a pastor, I was filled with anxiety about my lack of ability to do this. One day while reading the Bible, these words from Isaiah 41:10 became very helpful, "Do not fear, for I am with you; do not be afraid, for I am your God. I will strengthen you; I will help you; I will hold on to you with My righteous right hand." I have memorized these five "I ams" and "I wills" by letting my four fingers and thumb be reminders of them. My right hand is a symbol to me of Yahweh's "righteous right hand." This is my shield of faith.

Many times Satan has sent a flaming arrow of doubt regarding my ability to serve God; my response is the faith affirmation of Isaiah 41:10. This extinguishes the fiery missile and I have peace. I urge you to ask God to lead you to discover just the right words to build your own special shield from His Word.

Take the helmet of salvation (v.17a). The vital protection for our mind, our thought process, is listed next. Satan will attack our mind by seeking to plant thoughts that are displeasing to Yahweh. He does this because he knows our minds control our actions. As the writer of Proverbs declares, "As a person thinks in his heart, so is he" (Proverbs 23:7). Notice here the connection of the mind and heart; these terms refer to the same aspect of our personhood. Proverbs 4:23 gives this challenge: "Guard your heart above all else, for it is the source of life."

The best defense against the adversary's attempt to deceive our mind is "the helmet of salvation." The term *salvation* is used here in the broad sense of God's deliverance from all kinds of evil. His complete salvation begins with a new birth wherein we receive a new nature. Listen to Yahweh's words through Jeremiah about this: "I will make a new covenant . . . I will place My law within them and write it on their hearts. I will be their God, and they will be My people" (Jeremiah 31:31-33). The amazing truth about this new covenant is that His "law" within us is none other than the Spirit of Christ—the Holy Spirit! As Paul told the Corinthian believers, "Now we have not received the spirit of the world, but the Spirit who is from God, in order to know what has been feely given to us by God...we have the mind of Christ" (1 Corinthians 2:12, 16).

Think about that! **The mind of Christ is literally ours! His way of thinking and, therefore, His way of living belong to us.** Amazing, yet true! What is our role in using this part of armor? Paul says, "Take the helmet of salvation." *Take it* in the sense of claiming Yahweh's deliverance from all kinds of wrong thinking. *Take the helmet* in the sense of committing your mind and heart to His protection and control every day.

The sword of the Spirit, which is God's word (v. 17b). A Roman soldier had one primary offensive weapon—a short, sharp sword. He used his sword to attack and defeat his enemy in hand-to-hand combat. Like this soldier we are to engage the enemy for the purpose of winning, not merely surviving. So we must not just focus on defending ourselves against Satan's attacks; we are to be aggressive against him. Notice Paul's words at this point: "The weapons of our warfare are not fleshly, but are powerful through God for the demolition of strongholds. We demolish arguments and every high-minded thing that is raised up against the knowledge of God, taking every thought captive to the obedience of Christ" (2 Corinthians 10:4-5). Talk about being aggressive—consider these terms: "demolition of strongholds . . . demolish arguments . . . ." Sounds very proactive to me!

Remember our weapon for this fight is God's Word. Not our words, not our best efforts, not our schemes, but His Word, the Bible. Believers have often resorted to their own resources for dealing with the devil and found themselves to be no match for this powerful, crafty adversary. Peter said Satan is like a "roaring lion, looking for anyone he can devour" (1 Peter 5:8). Our best model for using God's word when dealing with the Devil is found in the temptation experience of Jesus.

Near the beginning of Jesus' ministry, just after His baptism, He was led by the Holy Spirit to spend 40 days fasting in a wilderness area. After a prolonged time without food, the Devil came to tempt Him. This adversary made three appeals, all very tempting. However, all attempts were contrary to the Father's plan for His Son. Jesus responded to each of Satan's appeals by quoting some biblical text. (Read this episode from Luke 4:1-13.) How difficult to even imagine the implications of this spiritual battle! If Satan could have deceived Jesus at this beginning point of His task, a huge victory would have been won for the powers of darkness.

Fortunately for all humankind, Jesus overcame each temptation, and His defeated enemy left Him for a short time. Jesus could have simply told the Devil to flee and the battle would have been over. He chose instead to leave an example of how we can win over this enemy. **Jesus used the sword of the Spirit, God's Word to resist and defeat every attempt of Satan.** The writer of Hebrews declares an impressive description of this weapon: "For the word of God is living and effective and sharper than any two-edged sword, penetrating as far as to divide soul, spirit, joints, and marrow; it is a judge of the ideas and thoughts of the heart" (Hebrews 4:12).

What a weapon God has placed at our disposal! How important for us to give time each day to become more familiar with this weapon and thus be prepared when the enemy attacks or when we choose to attack his strongholds. Consider an amazing story at this point. Some years ago my wife and I went to Oradea, Romania, to provide leadership training for several churches in that area. Our host was one of the pastors named Cornel Iova. Later, he visited our home in Tennessee and we have maintained a connection by email for a many years.

Cornel is a very bold preacher and travels to many cities in Romania to lead evangelistic crusades. He told me about this unusual happening in one of these places. The local orthodox priest heard about these meetings and warned his parishioners not to attend. He threatened to excommunicate them if they participated. The host pastor told Cornel about this action and cautioned him about this powerful religious figure.

On the opening night of their series of meetings, Cornel was seated on the platform beside the pastor, waiting for the time to begin the service. He noticed a man come through the doorway at the back of this small auditorium and sit on the back row. The pastor whispered to Cornel, "There is the priest I told you about; he is here to see if any of his people have come. You must be very careful about what you say." Cornel said he felt the Holy Spirit leading him to begin the service by recognizing this "honored guest" and to thank him for coming. Then, to the displeasure of the pastor, Cornel boldly invited the priest to come forward and have the opening prayer! With great reluctance this enemy walked slowly forward and recited some formal prayer, then sat down with obvious anger and embarrassment.

Cornel proceeded to preach a simple gospel message with unusual power. When he extended the invitation for hearers to repent of sin and come forward to receive Christ, to the amazement of everyone, this priest came! Cornel prayed with him and asked him to remain after the service.

The man's name was Seraphim Scrobut. He told Cornel he had never heard this message before and could not keep himself from responding. During the following days they continued counseling with him and encouraged him to return to his church and preach the same gospel, giving his own testimony of how he had recently been saved.

He did as they suggested and was soon removed from his position and turned out of the orthodox church. In time he became an effective preacher among evangelicals in that area. What a testimony to the power of God's Word—like a sword cutting to this man's heart and delivering him from the enemy!

Pray at all times in the Spirit (v. 18). Four references to prayer are made in the verses immediately following the parts of armor list. An old gospel song says, "Put on the gospel armor, each piece put on with prayer." We must daily claim this armor through prayer. Here is a suggested way to pray about this: *Gracious Yahweh Nissi, thank you for providing for my protection against Satan. Today I take the belt of Your truth, the breastplate of Your righteousness, the shoes of the gospel, the shield of faith, the helmet of salvation and the sword of Your Word. I depend on Your strength for the battle. Thank You for victory over Satan, the world, and the flesh today. Amen.*

The Certainty of Victory

I mentioned at the beginning of this chapter a man with a tattoo that read, "Born to lose." We who have been born-again are *born to win*! **Our victory is not in ourselves—not in trying harder or being more diligent; our victory is Jesus Christ.** Paul said it this way, "In all these things we are more than victorious through Him who loved us" (Romans 8:37). The apostle John echoed the same truth like this: "Whatever has been born of God conquers the world. This is the victory that has conquered the world: our faith. And who is the one who conquers the world but the one who believes that Jesus is the Son of God?" (1 John 5:4-5).

> Our victory is not in ourselves—not in trying harder or being more diligent; our victory is Jesus Christ.

Oliver Perry was the hero of the Battle of Lake Erie during the War of 1812. He is quoted as saying, "We have met the enemy, and they are ours." We, too, will meet enemies in spiritual warfare every day. But they are defeated enemies; Jesus Christ won the war against them on our behalf. We must claim by faith the victory. **What a difference a name makes—the difference between our defeat and His victory—Yahweh Nissi.**

STUDY GUIDE

Chapter Four: The Difference Between Our Defeat and His Victory

1. Recall a personal experience of spiritual defeat. How can such a loss be overcome?

2. Read Exodus 17:8-16. What did Moses name the altar (v. 15)?

3. Identify three enemies we engage in spiritual warfare.

    a.
    b.
    c.

    Which of these enemies causes you the most trouble? Why?

4. Read Ephesians 6:10-20. List the six parts of the Christian's armor.

    1.   4.

    2.   5.

    3.   6.

Select three parts of the armor that have received the least personal attention.

1.

2.

3.

How can these areas be strengthened?

5. Who makes the difference between victory and defeat in spiritual warfare?

CHAPTER FIVE

The Difference Between Being
Our Own and Being His

YAHWEH M'KADDESH
(YAH-way ma-CAD-esh)

O<small>NE OF THE MOST</small> fundamental and significant truths about Yahweh is the fact of His holiness. The psalmist declared, "Exalt Yahweh our God; bow in worship at His footstool. He is holy" (Psalm 99:5). The prophet Isaiah received a special revelation of Yahweh when he saw Him seated on His throne in the temple. Angels were standing above Him and they called out to one another, "Holy, holy, holy is Yahweh Sabaoth; His glory fills the whole earth" (Isaiah 6:3). More than 700 references to Yahweh's holiness are found in the Old Testament and many more in the New Testament.

The Hebrew word for holy is *qadash;* the Greek term is *hagios.* Both words convey the idea of someone or something being set apart, separated, dedicated, or consecrated. Various English terms come from this root, such as "holy," "sanctuary," "sanctified," "saint," "hallow," and others. **To say that Yahweh is holy means He is set apart from all His creation in the sense that He is different—He alone is God, and there is none other like Him**. No other is like Him in power—He alone creates something from nothing. No other is like Him in purity. He alone is without sin. No other is like Him in character. All virtue has its source in Him. Yahweh is *holy*!

Consider these references to the uniqueness of Yahweh as being holy:

"You [Israel] were shown these things so that you would know that Yahweh is God; there is none besides Him" (Deuteronomy 4:35).

"There is no one holy like Yahweh. There is no one besides You! And there is no rock like our God" (1 Samuel 2:2).

"This is what Yahweh, the King of Israel and its Redeemer, Yahweh Sabaoth, says, "I am the first and I am the last. There is no God but me" (Isaiah 44:6).

"There is no other God but Me, a righteous God and Savior; there is no one except Me. Turn to Me and be saved, all the ends of the earth. For I am God and there is no other" (Isaiah 45:21-22).

Notice the repetition of this fundamental truth: "I am God and there is no other." This reality is what sets Yahweh apart, makes Him holy, He is One of a kind—one true and living God. All other so called gods are the product of human and Satanic imagination.

In this chapter we will examine another combination name, one that focuses on the aspect of Yahweh's holiness. Several occurrences of this very special combination are featured. The first is found in Exodus 31:12-17. In this situation Yahweh gave Moses the concept of the *Sabbath*—a word meaning "rest." Here is the text: "Yahweh said to Moses: 'Tell the Israelites: You must observe My Sabbaths, for it is a sign between Me and you throughout your generations, so that you will know that I am Yahweh M'Kaddesh.'" *M'Kaddesh* comes from the root word for holy—"qadash." Thus God revealed Himself here as "**I AM the One Who sanctifies you—Who makes you holy.**" He went on to tell Moses that the Sabbath day would be a perpetual reminder to His people of just Who is their God.

"Observe the Sabbath, for it is holy to you. Whoever profanes it must be put to death. If anyone does work on it, that person must be cut off from his people. For six days work may be done, but on the seventh day there must be a Sabbath of complete rest, dedicated to Yahweh....The Israelites must observe the Sabbath, celebrating it throughout their generations as a perpetual covenant. It is a sign forever between Me and the Israelites, for in six days Yahweh made the heavens and the earth, but on the seventh day He rested and was refreshed" (vv. 14-17).

The second occurrence of this special name is found in Leviticus 20:7-8: "Consecrate yourselves and be holy, for I am Yahweh your God. Keep My statutes and do them; I am Yahweh M'Kaddesh." (Other references to Yahweh M'Kaddesh are Leviticus 21:8, 23; 22:9, 16 and 22.) Notice that in this instance Yahweh calls on His people to "be holy" even as He is holy. Thus **Yahweh reveals Himself as being holy and the One who makes His people holy**. Consider various aspects of life where Yahweh M'Kaddesh makes a difference.

A Different Owner

Each of us has a personal identity, who we are. But **more important than *who* we are is *whose* we are**. In fact *whose* we are will largely determine *who* we are. This fact was impressed upon me many years ago in a rather unusual way. My wife and I were students at the University of Oklahoma, living near the campus in an upstairs apartment owned by an older couple: Mr. and Mrs. J.S. Yowell. One spring morning I walked across the wide, screened-in front porch of this large house on my way to class. Mrs. Yowell was seated in a rocking chair at one end of the porch, doing some knitting. As I passed by, I greeted her and started out the screen door. She returned my greeting and said, "Now remember whose you are and whom you represent today." I paused to ask her to repeat what she said. "Oh, it's just something I always said to my children as they were leaving the house. I wanted them to remember that they belonged to the Lord and always represented Him wherever they were."

What wise counsel! And I have remembered those words ever since that morning. What she said is true for every follower of Jesus. The apostle Paul said it best, "Do you not know that your body is a sanctuary of the Holy Spirit who is in you, whom you have from God? You are not your own, for you were bought at a price; therefore glorify God in your body" (1 Corinthians 6:19-20). When our Lord died on the cross, He not only paid our sin debt, He purchased us. We literally belong to Him; He owns us!

Sometimes our words, as well as our actions, do not affirm His ownership. Since He owns us, He has the right to control us—to be Lord of us. Our role is that of a steward, a manager, of all He places in our possession. But we are not owners, just temporary custodians of that which is His. Yahweh M'Kaddesh is the One who makes this true; He sets us apart for Himself. For this reason the New Testament refers to believers as "saints," a word that comes from the same root as *qadash*—"holy." One interpreter said, "Everyone is either a saint or an ain't!" That is, either we are His (saints) or we ain't His!

Another New Testament term that expresses His ownership of us is "slaves" (*doulos* in Greek). This interesting word is used to describe believers some 40 times, while the Old Testament word for slaves (ebed) describes God people more than 250 times. These give a clear revelation of the fact that our relationship to Yahweh is one of His ownership and our obligation to serve Him. Slaves have no property rights, no control of their time or life—they are possessions of their master. What a difference this makes when we become aware that we have been purchased by the blood of Christ and are to be absolutely controlled by Him.

Recognizing His ownership makes a huge difference in our attitude toward ourselves, our possessions, and our accountability to Him. One way I have illustrated this truth when teaching others is to extend my hand, palm up, and say, "If we think of ourselves as owners, we open our hand to receive God's gifts, then close our hand to thank Him for what He gives for us to use as we please. But when we understand our role as stewards, we open our hand to receive all He gives and keep it open, saying, 'Thank you for entrusting this possession to me, I recognize that it is still yours and my hand remains open for you to control its use.'" What a difference!

A Different Lifestyle

Mrs. Yowell said, "Remember whom you represent." Again, Paul helps us with this concept when he wrote, "We are ambassadors for Christ" (2 Corinthians 5:20). When our son Mark was a boy, he belonged to a missions organization in our church called *Royal Ambassadors*. Their motto was this Bible verse and the explanation was: "An ambassador is one who represents the person of the king in the court of another." Mark was very serious about being Yahweh's ambassador and today Mark and his wife Judy are missionaries in Singapore.

A distinctive and unique lifestyle becomes ours when we are reborn and transformed by Christ. He calls us the "salt of the earth" and the "light of the world." Both word pictures speak of the powerful effect our lives should have on those around us. Recently, I have been reading a book by Joe Stowell entitled, *Jesus Nation*. Several times he speaks of the lifestyle of a Christian as being "counterintuitive." We all begin life with a sense of intuition—a natural insight into life situations, a perception of truth, a self-determined sense of values.

Stowell maintains that once we receive the Spirit of Christ, the Holy Spirit, we have a new sense of values, an awareness of ultimate truth. These values are often contrary to our former understanding; they are counterintuitive. The result is a lifestyle that contradicts that of this world. For example, our values are different, as is our behavior.

He tells about a professional golfer named Bernhard Langer who won the Masters tournament on Easter Sunday. He was interviewed by a reporter on national TV and asked if this was the greatest day in his life. He replied, "This is the greatest day in my golfing career, but it doesn't compare to the fact that two thousand years ago today my Lord and Savior died and rose again to give me eternal life." That is counterintuitive—contrary to the normal human sense of value!

If we are surrendered to Yahweh M'Kaddesh, He will manifest His lifestyle through our behavior and words in countless ways. The first followers of Jesus were not known as *Christians*, but as persons of The Way. This term is used in Acts 9 when Saul (later Paul) went to Damascus to arrest followers of Jesus. The text reads, "Meanwhile, Saul, still breathing threats and murder against the disciples of the Lord, went to the high priest and requested letters from him to the synagogues in Damascus, so that if he found any who belonged to **the Way**, whether men or women, he might bring them as prisoners to Jerusalem" (Acts 9:1-2).

How amazing that this zealous opponent of the Way ultimately became one of its greatest advocates! Later he expressed this miraculous change in these impressive words: "If anyone is in Christ, there is a new creation; old things have passed away, and look, new things have come" (2 Corinthians 5:17). The "old things" that have passed away include our former lifestyle—one of self-centeredness. The "new things" include a new lifestyle—one of Christ-centeredness. As Paul again stated, "For me, living is Christ and dying is gain" (Philippians 1:21).

You may have heard the story of the cowboy who would ride into town on Saturday night, tie up his horse in front of the local saloon and spend the evening drinking and gambling. The local pastor began praying for him, as did many other Christians. One Sunday morning he rode up to the church, hitched his horse to the rail and went inside. After several weeks of doing this, he was saved, baptized, and became a faithful member of the church. One of his old drinking companions asked him what happened. He replied, "Well sometime ago I came to know Jesus; He gave me a new life; now, I've changed hitchin' posts!" When we become hitched up to Jesus, others will notice a change in us—an entirely new lifestyle.

A Different Position

Sanctification affects us in two ways. First, our *condition*. Because we have a new life, His life, we manifest a new lifestyle. Second, our *position,* **our new Owner sets us apart to be His special people.** Look with me at the first mention of this gift. As Moses led his people out of bondage in Egypt and into the wilderness they came, after a three month journey, to Mount Sinai. Yahweh called for Moses to come up the mountain where He spoke these words, "Now if you will listen to Me and carefully keep My covenant, you will be My own possession out of all the peoples, although all the earth is Mine, and you will be My kingdom of priests and My holy nation" (Exodus 19:5-6).

The word *possession,* in this passage, comes from the Hebrew term *segullah,* meaning "a special treasure." The idea behind this word is that God considers all His creation to be of great value—a treasure. Within this vast treasure, He has something special—His segullah, His own chosen people. One interpreter expressed the meaning of segullah this way. Suppose your house was on fire and after getting your family out there was time to retrieve one material possession. That choice would be your segullah—your special treasure. (For me it would be a box of personal journals I have kept for over forty years.)

Yahweh M'Kaddesh has set apart His people from all others. All who know Him as Father, through faith in the Lord Jesus; all who have been spiritually born into His forever family are His "own possession." Notice that He calls us His "kingdom of priests and My holy nation." Here is the first biblical mention of both "possession" and "kingdom." What a privileged status we have as Yahweh's chosen people! We are special to Him as His redeemed people. Notice how Paul expressed this truth in his brief letter to Titus: "He gave Himself for us to redeem us from all lawlessness and to cleanse for Himself a special people, eager to do good works" (Titus 2:14).

Many studies have been conducted regarding the importance of a person having a proper self-esteem. Each of us needs to feel good about who we are. We are persons of value and significance. **Nothing affirms self-esteem more completely and accurately than the fact of being chosen as God's *segullah*—His special people.** When you are tempted to put yourself down because of some failure or someone's criticism, remember what Yahweh says about you being a person greatly treasured by Him. If you need further proof of this fact, remember the cross where Yahweh gave His Son to pay the penalty for our sin; what amazing love!

> *Nothing affirms self-esteem more completely and accurately than the fact of being chosen as God's segullah– His special people.*

An old gospel song conveys this truth in these memorable words:

I once was an outcast stranger on earth, a sinner by choice and an alien by birth.
But I've been adopted; my name's written down--
An heir to a mansion, a robe and a crown.
I'm a child of the King, a child of the King,
With Jesus my Savior, I'm a child of the King.

--Harriet E. Buell

A Different Temple

The benefits we enjoy as a "child of the King" are many. However none is more awesome than the fact that **our human bodies become the literal temple of the Spirit of Yahweh**. Prior to our new birth, our body is the temple of our human spirit. But when we receive Yeshua (Jesus) by faith, He comes to live within us by His Holy Spirit.

Listen to Paul's words about this miracle: "Don't you know that you are God's sanctuary and that the Spirit of God lives in you? If anyone ruins God's sanctuary, God will ruin him; for God's sanctuary is holy, and that is what you are" (1 Corinthians 3:16-17). Note the words "sanctuary" (3 times) and "holy." These terms come from the same root word meaning "that which is set apart." Later in this letter to the Corinthian Christians, Paul repeats the same truth: "Do you not know that your body is a sanctuary of the Holy Spirit who is in you, whom you have from God? You are not your own, for you were bought at a price; therefore glorify God in your body" (1 Corinthians 6:19-20).

The believers in Corinth lived in a very immoral culture; sexual sins of all kinds were very common. Paul was reminding these young converts that their bodies were different than those of unbelievers. Their bodies were temples for Yahweh. Therefore he warned them to keep away from immoral activities. Their bodies belonged to Yahweh. Again, Paul wrote "The body is not for sexual immorality but for the Lord, and the Lord for the body . . . should I take the members of Christ and make them members of a prostitute?" (1 Corinthians 6:13-15). We are accountable to God for the way we use His temple!

This truth becomes the highest motivation for maintaining good health habits. **Since our body is Yahweh's temple, we are His temple-keepers.** How essential is our role in seeking to keep His temple clean, fit, and pleasing to Him. My wife and I have a friend named Michael Flynt. He and his wife were members of the Sunday School class my wife taught for several years. Mike has always been concerned about his physical condition. As a young man he began lifting weights and exercising to keep himself in good shape. He was so driven by this passion for physical fitness that he invented an exercise device for home use. One day he came to our home, demonstrated this compact platform and gave his invention to us.

Many years later we read with much interest about his decision to return to college and complete his degree. His story made national news headlines. When Michael was a senior student at Sul Ross State University in Alpine, Texas, he was the captain of his football team. Early in the season he violated team rules and was expelled from school. This meant that he left with a year of eligibility remaining. One day years later he was talking with a friend about the regret he felt about his failure to complete his degree. This friend challenged him to apply for readmission and finish what he started.

After praying about this possibility, Mike decided to contact the school. He was granted admission. Then the thought came of completing his football career. He contacted the coach who was reluctant to permit someone his age to risk injury by playing such a demanding sport. However, Michael was persistent and the coach allowed him to participate in spring training. Because he had maintained a strong healthy body, Mike made the team and at 59 years of age became the oldest man to ever play on an NCAA football team. His recorded his amazing experience in a book entitled *The Senior*. (available at Amazon.com.)

Recently he shared information with me about a new program he is developing for adults called "Fit for a King: Rebuilding the Temple of God." His concept is based on the biblical story of Ezra rebuilding the temple in Jerusalem plus Paul's words in 1 Corinthians 6:19-20. Mike uses this as an illustration of how, through proper eating and exercise, we can rebuild our bodies as God's temple.

What about your physical condition—your temple for Yahweh? Consider the accountability we all have to present ourselves, body, soul, and spirit, for our Master's use. Some day we will be asked by Him how we cared for His temple.

Stuart Briscoe is one of my favorite authors. In one of his books about sanctification he states: **"Christianity is nothing less than all of Him in all of you."** That says it so well! Yahweh M'Kaddesh makes a profound, thorough difference in all who come to Him—the difference between belonging to ourselves or belonging body, soul, and spirit to Him.

> *"Christianity is nothing less than all of Him in all of you."*

***Suggested prayer*: Yahweh M'Kaddesh, You are holy. I worship You as the Holy One—set apart from all creation because You are different. Thank You for calling us to be holy, and for setting us apart for Yourself. I want your holiness to be more and more manifest in my mind, heart, and soul. Use me today as a witness of who You are and what a difference You alone can make in all who come to You. Amen.**

STUDY GUIDE

Chapter Five: The Difference Between
Being Our Own and Being His

1. In your opinion what is a holy person?

2. "More important than who we are is whose we are." Agree or Disagree? Why?

3. "If we are surrendered to Yahweh M'Kaddesh, He will manifest His lifestyle though our behavior and words in countless ways."

   Relate two personal examples of this truth.

   a.

   b.

4. In what ways are you God's special treasure?

5. Write four sentences to express what difference is made since you know your body is God's temple.

   a. physically

   b. mentally

   c. spiritually

   d. socially

CHAPTER SIX

The Difference Between Our Turmoil and His Peace

YAHWEH SHALOM
(YAH-way sha-LOME)

THE WORD "SHALOM" REMINDS me of an experience I had several years ago. I was part of a team of volunteer construction workers who traveled to Guatemala City, Guatemala, to help build a worship center for the Shalom Baptist Church. Later, several members of that team organized the Shalom Foundation, a group of interested lay persons who wanted to continue and expand the ministry of helping that congregation. Today the Shalom Foundation has broadened its outreach to include the renovation and staffing of a hospital for children in Guatemala City.

I mention these facts to help explain the full meaning of *shalom*. This term is one of many that cannot be adequately translated by any single English word. Just as the Shalom Foundation is seeking to minister to physical, spiritual, emotional, and relational needs of persons, so this word is all inclusive of these areas of personal need. Various English terms are included in "shalom", such as health, prosperity, peace, wholeness, fulfillment, and completeness. One Bible dictionary states that "shalom" represents one of the most prominent theological concepts in the Old Testament. A respected scholar sums up the meaning this way: **"Shalom means that kind of peace that results from being a whole person in right relationship to God and to one's fellow man."**

> *"Shalom means that kind of peace that results from being a whole person in right relationship to God and to one's fellow man."*

Thus we understand why Jews have chosen this term that is so rich in meaning to use as a common greeting. When a Jewish person greets another, the terms used are: "Shalom aleichem," meaning "peace be unto you." The proper response is to reverse the words and say, "Aleichem shalom," meaning "unto you be peace." The blessing conveyed by this simple greeting is that of personal completeness as a result of living in harmony with God.

The combination of "Yahweh" and "Shalom" occurs once in the Bible. You may recall the account of Yahweh calling a young man named Gideon to deliver His people from their enemies, the Midianites. This narrative is found in the book of Judges, a record of approximately 400 years in the history of the Israelite people. During this troublesome time, Yahweh's chosen people, Israel, were like sheep without a shepherd. One description of their condition is found in these sad words, "After them [those of the generation following Joshua] another generation rose up who did not know Yahweh or the works He had done for Israel. The Israelites did what was evil in Yahweh's sight. They worshiped the Baals and abandoned Yahweh, the God of their fathers" (Judges 2:10-11).

This period of the Judges has been called a time of "chaotic restlessness." Yahweh sought to help His people by calling out a series of judges; some turned out to be good, while most were not. One of these chosen leaders was a young man named Gideon. Yahweh called him while he was secretly threshing wheat in order to hide the grain from the enemy. The command was to "Go in the strength you have and deliver Israel from the power of Midian" (Judges 6:14). In response to Yahweh's call, Gideon asked for a special sign. He wanted some kind of visible affirmation of this divine commission. When Gideon brought an offering of a young goat and unleavened bread, he was instructed to place them on a rock. A fire suddenly came out of the rock and consumed the entire offering. Then Yahweh spoke to Gideon saying, "Peace (shalom) to you. Don't be afraid, for you will not die." Gideon responded by building an altar to Yahweh and calling it **Yahweh Shalom** ("Yahweh is peace."). (See Judges 6:23-24.) This demonstration was Gideon's way of affirming the hope that Yahweh would bring total prosperity to His people, including deliverance from enemies as well as restoring a right relationship with Him.

71

Sure enough, Yahweh used this young, unproven novice to bring an amazing and miraculous deliverance of His people. Remember how Gideon assembled an army of 32,000 men to defeat the enemy? After Yahweh guided him to reduce this force, Gideon was left with 300 choice soldiers who were given the victory. This event revealed Yahweh as the ultimate source of *shalom*—true prosperity and peace. From this remarkable revelation, Yahweh shows that He is the answer to humankind's quest for a life characterized by true satisfaction and fulfillment.

The term "shalom" occurs more than 170 times in the Old Testament. The New Testament word for peace is "eirene." Examine several of these notable references as they apply to our needs today. As we look at each one, ask yourself if you are claiming this benefit for yourself and others. We begin with the way to find this peace.

HOW TO DISCOVER PEACE

In 1953 Billy Graham wrote a widely read book: *Peace with God.* In the opening chapter he said, "All humanity is seeking the answer to the confusion, the moral sickness, the spiritual emptiness that oppresses the world. All mankind is crying out for guidance, for comfort, for peace." He went on to explain how the answer to this dilemma is found only through a right relationship with God through faith in Jesus Christ.

The prophet Isaiah lived over 2700 years ago and made the same declaration in these words: "The result of righteousness will be peace [shalom]; the effect of righteousness will be quiet confidence forever" (Isaiah 32:17). **True peace begins with a right relationship with God; apart from this there is no lasting peace.** Contrary to this present world's system of values, genuine peace of mind and heart will never come in an ongoing manner from anything this world offers. **All the treasures and pleasures of this world will not bring true peace.**

Consider these words of Jesus, the Prince of Peace: "Peace I leave with you. My peace I give to you. I do not give to you as the world gives. Your heart must not be troubled or fearful" (John 14:27). He spoke these words during the final hours before His death on the cross. His disciples were extremely troubled and fearful, both for Him and for themselves. These men had left everything to follow Him and now it appeared their dreams of ruling over Israel with Him as their Messiah were ending. What would they do without Him?

You may have faced similar situations where you felt abandoned by God, left alone without hope. Sometimes Yahweh allows these times of agonizing distress in order to teach us lessons we can learn in no other way. Following Jesus' words of comfort found in John 14, He spoke for the first time about the ministry of the Holy Spirit, whom He said the Father would send after Jesus went away. Among other things, Jesus said the Holy Spirit would be with them to teach them, guide them, reveal what is to come, and be their personal Counselor. Jesus' final words on this subject were: "I have told you these things so that in Me you may have peace. You will have suffering in the world. Be courageous! I have conquered the world" (John 16:33).

Jesus is the ultimate peace-giver! Apart from Him no true and lasting peace exists. But how do we connect to this Source? Listen to this wise counsel from the apostle Paul, "Therefore since we have been declared righteous by faith, we have peace with God through our Lord Jesus Christ" (Romans 5:1). When, by faith, we call upon the Lord Jesus to save us from our sins, Yahweh declares us to be righteous, meaning we are given a right relationship with Him. The war is over; our hostility against Yahweh is ended; peace has come! We no longer live as Yahweh's enemies, separated from Him because of our sins. He literally adopts us into His forever family, as well as gives us a new nature—one that loves and obeys Him.

I have known many individuals who made this amazing discovery. Hughie Davison was a typical oil field "rough neck." He gambled, drank excessively, had a bad habit of cursing, and was given to immoral behavior. None of his activities brought peace of mind; he was tormented by his corrupt life style. The first time I met him was one Sunday morning in Hobbs, New Mexico, when he showed up at our morning worship service—looking for help. He listened closely as I proclaimed the gospel message, and this troubled man responded as a "seeker." At the close of the service I asked any who wanted to make some commitment to Christ or needed help with their relationship with Him or His church to come forward. Hughie walked all the way from the back of the church, threw his big arms around me and said, "I need God!" We helped him understand the good news of how he could begin a new life through faith in Jesus.

In a relatively short time Hughie became a completely new person. His old habits were laid aside and he fell in love with the Lord and His Word. The peace he longed for was the most exciting discovery of his first 55 years of life. He lived his remaining 20 years as a different person, all because of his relationship with *Yahweh Shalom* and the people of shalom. When I think of Hughie, I remember these words of truth: "Therefore if anyone is in Christ, there is a new creation; old things have passed away, and look, new things have come. Now everything is from God, who reconciled us to Himself through Christ and gave us the ministry of reconciliation" (2 Corinthians 5:17-18).

Perhaps you have never experienced this miracle of grace. Let me urge you to turn from seeking your own way to finding a life of meaning and happiness. Admit your failures to Yahweh as you call upon Him for forgiveness, restoration, and the peace that comes from a right relationship with Him. I promise you that He will hear your plea and answer in His own amazing way.

HOW TO MAINTAIN PEACE

If you have been a Christian for very long, you know that discovering peace with God is one thing; maintaining this same peace is an additional challenge. This is true because we are sinners before we are saved by grace, and continue to live with our sinful nature afterwards. **Being born again means we now have two natures, an old one that rebels against God, and a new nature that agrees with God, desiring to please Him.** Times occur when all of us will lapse into sinful attitudes and actions; the result will be the loss of peace with God. What should we do? The Apostle John gives a clear answer: "If we confess our sins, He is faithful and righteous to forgive us our sins and to cleanse us from all unrighteousness" (1 John 1:9). From a long life of experience with these matters I have learned the importance of "keeping short accounts" with God. By this I mean do not allow a day to end without confessing every known sinful thought and deed to Him. I claim by faith His forgiveness and cleansing—just as He promises. Then I begin each new day with thanksgiving for His gracious pardon for the past as well as His power for overcoming the old nature in the new day.

In addition to this practice of dealing with sins, **we must learn to practice spiritual disciplines that help suppress the old nature and express the new nature.** Think about this prayer: "You will keep in perfect peace the mind that is dependent on You, for it is trusting in You. Trust in Yahweh forever, because in Yahweh, Yahweh is everlasting peace" (Isaiah 26:3-4). In the Hebrew language no terms are used such as *good, better, best* to express levels of benefit. We say something is good, another is better, but something else is best. The Hebrews expressed this gradation by simply repeating the same word. For example, when Isaiah had his vision of Yahweh in the temple, an angel declared, "Holy, holy, holy is Yahweh Sabaoth" (Isaiah 6:3). This repetition of "holy" raises this virtue to its highest level.

In a similar manner, the term "perfect peace" in Isaiah 26:3 is literally *shalom, shalom.* How do we maintain perfect peace? The prophet gives the answer in these words: "You will keep in shalom shalom *the mind that is dependent on You, for it is trusting in You.*" In order to keep this perfect peace we must mentally affirm our trust in and dependence on Yahweh. This discipline means that no matter what situation we are facing, whether it seems good or bad, pleasant or painful, we depend on His resources rather than our own. A.T. Pierson, a wise Christian leader, said, **"The peace of God is that eternal calm which lies far too deep in the praying, trusting soul to be reached by any external disturbances."**

We learn to be a "trusting soul" by consistently feeding on God's Word, the Bible. The apostle Paul declared, "So faith [trust] comes from what is heard and what is heard comes through the message of Christ" (Romans 10:17). No adequate substitute can be made for the discipline of opening the Bible every day and allowing the Holy Spirit to feed your faith. Consider this interesting statement from the psalmist regarding the relationship between biblical truth and peace: "Abundant peace belongs to those who love Your instruction; nothing makes them stumble" (Psalm 119:165). Divine "instruction" comes primarily as our Teacher, the Holy Spirit, gives clear counsel to us through the inspired textbook, the Bible. The class meets whenever we are willing to give the Teacher our attention, open the textbook, and allow Him to instruct us in the school of life.

Years ago I heard this interesting story: An American Indian came to faith in Christ and was asked by a friend to explain what happened. He replied, "I used to have a bad dog in my chest and this dog cause me to do bad things. When I accepted Jesus, He put a good dog in my chest who helps me do good. But sometimes these two dogs fight one another." His friend asked, "Which dog wins?" The Indian said, "The one I feed!" Are you daily feeding the new nature God has place within you—the nature of shalom?

HOW TO EXTEND PEACE

True followers of the Prince of Peace, will do more than enjoy the peace He gives. They will actively seek to share this full and meaningful life with others. Our Lord said, "Blessed are the peacemakers, because they will be called sons of God" (Matthew 5:9). This word "peacemaker" occurs only here in the Bible What does it mean? **We become peacemakers when we take the initiative to reach out to those who lack peace and seek to help them discover true peace—peace with God, with themselves, and with others.**

A biblical example of peacemaking is found in the apostle Paul's letter to the believers in the church at Philippi. Apparently two women in this fellowship were having some kind of conflict. Paul sought to be a peacemaker when he wrote: "I urge Euodia and I urge Syntyche to agree in the Lord. Yes, I also ask you, true partner, to help these women who have contended for the gospel at my side . . . ." (Philippians 4:2-3). Paul wanted these former co-workers of his to overcome their differences and experience a peaceful relationship.

You may recall an earlier time in Paul's ministry when he had such an intense disagreement with Barnabas that they "parted company" (Acts 15:36-41). Barnabas wanted to take young John Mark with them on their second missionary venture, but Paul remembered how Mark had had turned back on their first trip. Later Paul and Mark were reconciled and Paul wrote these interesting words to Timothy: "Make every effort to come to me soon . . . Bring Mark with you, for he is useful to me in the ministry" (2 Timothy 4:9, 11).

Even the best among us have times of conflict and disagreement. Thus we lose the peace of a good relationship. However, through love and forgiveness peace can and should be restored. **We must focus on being**

peacemakers not peace breakers. Every believer is called and sent to extend shalom to others. As we do this, we will be known as "sons of God" for He is the ultimate Peacemaker.

What a difference this name makes: **Yahweh Shalom**. Through faith in Him we find the grace and mercy that provides peace for us and through us to a most needy world. Join me in this prayer:

Suggested prayer: **Gracious God, our Yahweh Shalom. We bless Your most holy and helpful Name. Thank You for being our peace, the peace that passes all understanding. We do not understand how You can be so merciful to us. But we celebrate the completeness You give to us through Your Son, the Prince of Peace. Thank You for sending peacemakers to us who showed us the way to be reconciled to You. Now we ask that You use us to extend this wonderful peace to others, beginning in our own family and church. Amen.**

STUDY GUIDE

Chapter Six: The Difference Between Our Turmoil and His Peace

1. Read Judges 6:14-24. Express in your own words the meaning of "shalom."

2. How did you come to know *Yahweh Shalom* in a personal way?

3. Shalom (peace) is maintained by practicing certain spiritual disciplines. One example is that of learning to pray effectively. What other disciplines will help?

4. Describe a time when you made a difference by being a peacemaker.

CHAPTER SEVEN

The Difference Between Our Sin and God's Righteousness

YAHWEH TSIDKENU
(YAH-way tsid-KAY-nu)

L ET'S BEGIN THIS CHAPTER by looking at the contrast between our sin and Yahweh's righteousness. First, consider our sin. **The good news of the gospel can never adequately be appreciated until we understand the bad news of our natural human condition.** As one writer has stated, "The good news is so good because the bad news is so bad." The apostle Paul gives the clearest description of our total depravity in the early chapters of his letter to the Romans.

As we begin reading these verses I remember my friend Bud Williams, who once worked as a door-to-door salesman. He was an avid witness for Christ, always seeking opportunities to share the good news with others. If he entered a home and saw a crucifix on the wall, he knew this was probably a Catholic family. Wanting to be sure they understood the basic nature of the biblical plan of salvation, he would ask: "Have you ever read about the four 'nones' in the Bible?" They assumed he was referring to *nuns* like the ones they knew about. If they showed interest, he would open his New Testament to Romans 3 and read these words: "There is <u>none</u> righteous, no, not one; there is <u>none</u> who understands; there is <u>none</u> who seeks after God . . . .There is <u>none</u> who does good, no, not one" (Romans 3:10-12). Then he would go on to share the remainder of the gospel message.

These "nones" tell the story of our sinfulness in God's sight. Think of the best person you have ever known. You might assume that person would be acceptable to God and go to heaven when they die, just because of their good qualities. Not so! No one, not even the best of us, has escaped the reality of personal sin. "All have sinned and fall short of the glory of God" (Romans 3:23). Yes, some individuals live a very good, virtuous life and do many charitable deeds, but each of them at one time or another has chosen to rebel against God and disobey Him.

We learn the true nature of sin from the first persons who ever sinned—Adam and Eve. They were created as perfect human beings, completely innocent before God. However, God gave them the power to make choices and they were free to choose to obey or disobey Him. He said, "You are free to eat from any tree of the garden, but you must not eat from the tree of the knowledge of good and evil, for on the day you eat from it, you will certainly die" (Genesis 2:16-17). Apparently, Yahweh desired that His creation not have the knowledge of what was evil, but He allowed Adam and Eve to make that choice for themselves, a choice based on their trust in Him. Thus this first couple was fully aware of the consequences of choosing to ignore God's warning. However when faced with temptation, they used their freedom to make selfish choices; they rebelled against Yahweh, choosing their way rather than His.

The consequence of their transgression was severe and far-reaching. In fact, all nature and all humankind were affected by their decision to sin against Yahweh. The most serious punishment was to be separated from that close fellowship with Him they previously enjoyed. Their close communion with Yahweh died the day they sinned. No longer could they walk with Him in His paradise on earth. (See Genesis 3:22-24.)

Every person who has lived on earth since Adam and Eve, with the exception of Jesus, has followed their shameful example. **We have all chosen our way rather than that of Yahweh, and have all been separated from fellowship with Him.** Adam and Eve are not to blame for our sin, nor can the blame be passed to Satan who tempts us just as he did them. **We each make our own choice to rebel against God.** Therefore, we are guilty of sin and must face the consequence of our disobedience. As stated earlier, "There is none righteous, no, not one." This fact is the **bad news** for us: not only are we unrighteous before God, there is nothing we can do to become righteous--to blot out our record of guilt and be reconciled to Him.

Are you ready for some **good news**, some very, very good news? Think about it this way: Yahweh faced a divine dilemma, He created humankind for fellowship with Himself. But His creation consistently chose to go away from Him. He remains righteous, but everyone else is unrighteous. As the psalmist declared, ". . . no one alive is righteous in Your sight" (Psalm 143:2). Thus He made the only choice love can make. He took the initiative to provide a way for each person to be forgiven for sin, be re-created in His holy image, and be reconciled to Him. Yahweh chose to do this in spite of its tremendous cost—the cost of giving His only begotten Son to become a sacrifice for the sin of all humankind. Paul expressed this amazing act of grace like this:

"While we were still helpless, at the appointed moment, Christ died for the ungodly. For rarely will someone die for a just person—though for a good person perhaps someone might even dare to die. But God proves His own love for us in that while we were still sinners Christ died for us! Much more then, since we have now been declared righteous by His blood, we will be saved through Him from wrath. For if, while we were enemies, we were reconciled to God through the death of His Son, then how much more, having been reconciled, will we be saved by His life! And not only that, but we also rejoice in God through our Lord Jesus Christ, through whom we have now received reconciliation" (Romans 5:6-11).

Good news!! **Our sinfulness and all that our sinfulness deserves can be exchanged for Yahweh's righteousness and all that His righteousness provides for us.** Here is where one of His special combination names makes such a difference. This name is *Yahweh Tsidkenu*, a term found two times in the Old Testament, both in the book of Jeremiah. Let's examine these expressions.

> *Our sinfulness and all that our sinfulness deserves can be exchanged for Yahweh's righteousness and all that His righteousness provides for us.*

1. Jeremiah 23:5-6. Yahweh spoke to Jeremiah at a time when the people of Judah were about to be carried away to Babylon as captives. A very dark period of history for God's chosen people is recorded. But listen to these words of hope given to the prophet: "The days are coming—this is Yahweh's declaration—when I will raise up a righteous Branch of David. He will reign wisely as king and administer justice and righteousness in the land. In His days Judah will be saved, and Israel will dwell securely. This is what He will be named: "**Yahweh Is Our Righteousness**." [In Hebrew this name is *Yahweh Tsidkenu*.]

2. Jeremiah 33:16. The same basic message of 23:5-6 is repeated with one interesting exception: "Look, the days are coming—this is the Yahweh's declaration—when I will fulfill the good promises that I have spoken concerning the house of Israel and the house of Judah. In those days and at that time I will cause a Branch of righteousness to sprout up for David, and He will administer justice and righteousness in the land. In those days Judah will be saved, and Jerusalem will dwell securely, and this is what she will be named: "**Yahweh Is Our Righteousness**." [*Yahweh Tsidkenu*]

Notice the repetition in these two passages of the terms "righteous" and "righteousness." The Hebrew root of these words means "to be straight," and implies truthfulness, moral uprightness, integrity, and faithfulness. A similar term often associated with righteousness is justice, such as this reference: "Yahweh reigns! Let the earth rejoice…righteousness and justice are the foundation of His throne" (Psalm 97:1-2). Righteousness is a basic aspect of Yahweh's character. He is righteous and always acts in a righteous manner.

Now, look back to those two references from Jeremiah. Notice the promises concerning the coming of a "Branch of David" and a "Branch of righteousness." Who is this "branch"? These promises find their fulfillment in Jesus, a direct descendent (branch) of David, and who is described as the "Holy and Righteous One" (Acts 3:13-14). Yahweh's righteousness is more than a virtue, it is a Person. **Jesus, alone, of all persons who ever lived or shall live on this earth is perfectly righteous. For this reason**

He could become the substitute for all sinners; He had no sin debt of His own to pay, therefore He could pay our debt.

Paul sums up this truth in these powerful words: "He [*Yahweh*] made the One who did not know sin [Jesus]to be sin for us, so that we might become the righteousness of God in Him" (2 Corinthians 5:21). Think like this: **Yeshua (Jesus) is the righteousness of God. When we are in Him, we become the righteousness of God, not because of who we are, but because of *who* He is and *whose* we are—His!** This leads us to consider two aspects of righteousness, imputed righteousness and imparted righteousness.

IMPUTED RIGHTEOUSNESS

Since the Bible clearly declares that none of us is righteous by our own merit or works, the only way for us to obtain a right standing with God is by His gift, His grace. Paul uses the example of Abraham to show us how this is possible. In Romans 4:3 the apostle reminds his readers of this fact: "Abraham believed God, and it was credited to him for righteousness." The term "credited" translates a Greek word meaning "to reckon, to put down to one's account, to impute." Because Abraham exercised faith in Yahweh's promises to him, he was considered to be righteous before Yahweh. This right standing was God's gift based on Abraham's faith, and not something he achieved by good deeds. Paul went on to state: ". . . to the one who . . . believes on Him who declares righteous the ungodly, his faith is credited for righteousness . . . . Therefore, since we have been declared righteous by faith, we have peace with God through our Lord Jesus Christ" (Romans 4:5; 5:1).

The only hope we sinners have of ever being accepted by Yahweh is found here. He promises to impute the righteousness of Yeshua to our account, not on the basis of anything we have done but due to the fact that His Son died to pay the penalty for our sin. When we, by faith, accept this gracious offer, we are pardoned and restored to fellowship with Yahweh.

Paul refers to this gift as "having been justified" (Romans 5:1). Both "righteousness" and "justification" come from the same root word in Greek. **Yahweh declares us to be righteous or justified when we receive the Lord Jesus, who is in Himself our righteousness.**

An additional outcome of this imputed righteousness is known in Paul's writings as "reconciliation." This means that we, who once were separated and alienated from Yahweh due to our sin, are now fully restored to fellowship with Him; we are reconciled. As Paul states: "For if while we were enemies, we were reconciled to God through the death of His Son, then how much more, having been reconciled, will be saved by His life! And not only that, but we also rejoice in God through our Lord Jesus Christ through whom we have now received reconciliation" (Romans 5:10-11).

Apart from Christ, a long list of "debts" must be paid to Yahweh—debts accumulated each time we sin. Jesus paid for those debts when He died in our place upon the cross. Now those debts are PAID IN FULL and our record is clean. An old gospel song describes this transaction in these words:

There was a time on earth when in the book of Heaven
An old account was standing for sins yet unforgiv'n.
My name was at the top, and many things below,
I went unto the Keeper, and settled long ago.

Long ago, long ago,
Yes, the old account was settled long ago.
And the record's clear today, for He washed my sins away.
When the old account was settled long ago.

F.M. Graham

IMPARTED RIGHTEOUSNESS

Suppose you were in prison, serving a sentence for some crime. And suppose the judge decided to set you free with a clean record, completely forgiven. A pardon has been imputed to you. Good news! Just one problem, you would walk out of prison the same kind of person who went in. You would have the same nature that resulted in your crime. Now apply this to having righteousness imputed to us in a spiritual sense. Once we are justified, forgiven for all our transgressions against God, we are considered to be righteous as far as the record of our sin is concerned, but we need something more. We need a new nature.

Yahweh knows all about our sinful nature. He knows a completely new nature is needed, one characterized by righteousness rather than sin. Thus

He imparts His own righteous nature to us through regeneration—the gift of a new nature, His own holy nature. We are born again spiritually! Listen to these words from Simon Peter, a man who desperately needed a new nature: "As the One who called you is holy, you also are to be holy in all your conduct; for as it is written, 'Be holy, because I am holy'. . . . For you know that you were redeemed from your empty way of life inherited from the fathers...love one another earnestly from a pure heart, since **you have been born again**—not of perishable seed but of imperishable—through the living and enduring word of God" (1 Peter 1:15-23). In his second letter Peter states, "His divine power has given us everything required for life and godliness . . . . He has given us very great and precious promises, so that through them **you may share in the divine nature**, escaping the corruption that is in the word because of evil desires" (2 Peter 1:3-4).

These words clearly reveal the fact that we who have been justified through faith in Jesus Christ are called to live a distinctively new lifestyle, one of holiness, a Christ-like life. Yahweh makes this possible by giving us a new divine nature—the very nature of Christ. As Paul declared, ". . . I no longer live, but Christ lives in me. The life I now live in the flesh, I live by faith in the Son of God, who loved me and gave Himself for me" (Galatians 2:20). How can Christ be in heaven at the right hand of Yahweh and also be in us? This miracle happens when, at our new birth, Yahweh sends His Holy Spirit, the Spirit of Christ, to permanently take up residence in us. Paul refers to this truth in these words: "If anyone does not have the Spirit of Christ, he does not belong to Him. Now if Christ is in you, the body is dead because of sin, but the Spirit is life because of righteousness" (Romans 8:9-10).

None of us can live the Christian life apart from the life of Christ in us. His Holy Spirit produces all the Christ-like virtues in and through us. Paul spoke of the "fruit of the Spirit" being love, joy, peace, patience, kindness, goodness, faith, gentleness, and self-control (Galatians 5:22). The character of Jesus is on display through us, by means of the Holy Spirit's control. Here is the imparted righteousness of **Yahweh Tsidkenu** revealed in us.

> *None of us can live the Christian life apart from the life of Christ in us. His Holy Spirit produces all the Christ-like virtues in and through us.*

My friend, this wonder is the ultimate distinctive of Christianity. Here is what sets this way of life apart from all religions. In the truest sense of the word, Christianity is not a *religion*. Authentic Christianity is a *relationship* with the only true and living God. All religions focus on human effort. God's Word calls us to focus on divine effort, what Yahweh has done and is doing in all who choose to follow Him.

Let me illustrate this truth. Recently, I talked with a man who said he was Persian. He told me his story of coming to American many years ago. When I asked his name, he said, "My name is Mo." I replied, "As in Mohammed?" He affirmed that his parents named him from the prophet Mohammed. I asked if he followed that religion and worshiped at a mosque. He said, "My religion is to live by the Golden Rule." As we parted, I gave him some Christian literature. Since then I have prayed that God might open His eyes to the truth.

Mo's story is so similar to most people. No matter what their religion may be called, their hope is based on their own effort—that is, just seek to live a good life, treat people the way you want to be treated, and maybe you will end up in Paradise. Unfortunately for them, **no one can reach heaven by their own efforts, no matter how good they may be**. As Jesus declared, "I am the way, the truth, and the life. No one comes to the Father except through Me." (John 14:6).

An old gospel song speaks this truth:

My hope is built on nothing less than Jesus' blood and righteousness;
I dare not trust the sweetest frame, but wholly lean on Jesus' Name.

When He shall come with trumpet sound, O may I then in Him be found,
Dressed in His righteousness alone, faultless to stand before the throne.

On Christ, the Solid Rock, I stand—
All other ground is sinking sand, all other ground is sinking sand.

--Edward Mote

What is our role in this new quality of life? Not to be the producers of this life, but the receivers and the conveyers. **Our role is to cease *trying***

to live the righteous life on our own, and begin *trusting* Him to live His life through us. By continuously yielding control of ourselves to Him, this miracle happens. Paul called for this commitment when he wrote: "Therefore, brothers, by the mercies of God, I urge you to present your bodies as a living sacrifice, holy and pleasing to God; this is your spiritual worship. Do not be conformed to this age, but be transformed by the renewing of your mind, so that you may discern what is the good, pleasing, and perfect will of God" (Romans 12:1-2).

Here is a personal discipline that has greatly helped me in this matter. Years ago, I came across this prayer and each morning I begin the day with this heart-felt commitment:

> **Master, I want this day to be a day of Your control;**
> **To know the lordship of Your love triumphant in my soul,**
> **And all my longings, all my cares upon that love to roll.**
>
> **I want to know Your fellowship more fully all the way**
> **And in its bright reality to walk with You this day—**
> **Losing my life, that in Your life God's will shall be my stay.**
>
> **I want to prove, as Spirit taught, the power of Jesus' Name**
> **In it to work, in it to pray, in it each promise claim,**
> **As victors did who by Your blood once fought and overcame.**
>
> **O Master, make these wants to be unto fulfillment brought,**
> **And day by day unto Yourself lead captive every thought.**
> **Then shall at evensong be praise for all that God has wrought.**
> **Amen.**

I strongly recommend that you begin each day with a similar commitment. I promise that Yahweh will hear and honor such a surrender to His control. **Whatever we commit to Him, He keeps!** Remember, He alone is *Yahweh Tsidkenu*, the One who can declare us to be righteous, and then produce His righteous life in and through us. What a difference!

STUDY GUIDE

Chapter Seven: The Difference Between
Our Sin and God's Righteousness

1. Why does this chapter state that our sin is bad news?

2. How is *Yahweh Tsidkenu* good news for us?

3. State your understanding of "imputed righteousness" and "imparted righteousness."

4. What must we do to reflect Yahweh's righteousness? (See Galatians 2:20 for help)

5. List the name of someone you know in whom *Yahweh Tsidkenu* is making a difference between sin and righteousness.

CHAPTER EIGHT

The Difference Between Our Aloneness and His Presence

YAHWEH SHAMMAH
(YAH-way SHAM-mah)

O F ALL THE COMBINATION names for Yahweh, this one is the most significant for us. Why would I make this strong statement? Simply because no matter who Yahweh is—Provider, Healer, Overcomer, and all the others we have considered—unless He is **present with us**, none of these make a big difference for us in the here and now. The meaning of *Yahweh Shammah* **is: I AM THERE, which declares that He is with us; He is present—always!**

Let's begin our study with the only biblical reference to this combination which occurs in the final verse of Ezekiel. This prophet was an Israelite priest who was taken as a captive over 500 miles away to Babylon in 597 B.C., along with King Jehoiachin and 10,000 others (2 Kings 24:14-16). Ezekiel was about 25 years old at this time. Several years later, while living by the river Chebar which flowed from the Euphrates River, he was given a series of visions from God. He became the only Israelite prophet to carry out a ministry outside Israel's homeland.

Ezekiel boldly accused Yahweh's people of losing His favor due to their sins, primarily the sin of idolatry and forsaking His laws. However, after the fall of Jerusalem and the destruction of the temple in 586 B.C., Ezekiel's message to the exiles became one of hope. He assured the people of Yahweh's plan to restore His people back to their homeland, rebuild the temple and the city of Jerusalem. A key phrase, repeated 70 times in his book is: "Then they shall know that I am Yahweh."

The prophet's final message came in 571 B.C. He concluded with the description of a restored Jerusalem, making this promise: "The perimeter of the city will be six miles and the name of the city from that day on will be *YAHWEH SHAMMAH* (Yahweh is there.)" (Ezekiel 48:35). Thirty-three years later, King Cyrus surprised the people when he issued a decree in 538 B.C. permitting the Judeans to return home and rebuild the temple. More than 40,000 exiles accepted this offer.

Think about the significance of the city being known as *Yahweh Shammah*. These exiles were convinced that Yahweh had forsaken them. But such was not the case. Actually the people had forsaken Yahweh. Their years of suffering came as a direct consequence of their sinful idolatry. Now Yahweh was showing mercy and grace by restoring them to their homeland. The assurance that He would be with them as they returned to Judah was extremely comforting. We should not be surprised at this divine initiative. Consider a brief survey of biblical truth regarding Yahweh's revelation of Himself as One who is determined to be present with His people.

Yahweh's Persistent Presence

Beginning in Genesis 1:1 and continuing throughout the Bible is the fact of Yahweh's personal, direct involvement with His creation. Unlike other religions where their god is remote and must be sought and found by adherents, **the God of the Bible is persistently taking the initiative toward all humankind.** For example, we see Him not only creating Adam and Eve but also walking with them in the garden and communing with them.

Page after page of Scripture reveals His determination to reach fallen humankind as He faithfully pursued His plan to restore sinners from their broken relationship with Him. All the patriarchs were visited by Him; all were given the privilege of communicating with Him and being a part of His redemptive design. Consider a few of these episodes.

o   "Enoch walked with God 300 years" (Genesis 5:22).
o   "Noah walked with God" (Genesis 6:9).

o "When Abram was 99 years old, Yahweh appeared to him, saying, 'I am God Almighty. Live in My presence and be devout. I will establish My covenant between Me and you, and I will multiply you greatly'" (Genesis 17: 1-2).

o "Yahweh appeared to Isaac and said, 'I will be with you and bless you'" (Genesis 26:3).

o "Yahweh was standing there beside Jacob, saying, 'I am Yahweh. . . I am with you and will watch over you wherever you go . . . .'" (Genesis 28:13, 15).

o "Yahweh was with Joseph, and he became a successful man" (Genesis 39:2).

o Yahweh said to Moses, " I will dwell among the Israelites and be their God, who brought them out of the land of Egypt, so that I might dwell among them. I am Yahweh their God" (Exodus 29:46).

o "Yahweh spoke to Joshua . . . 'I will be with you, just as I was with Moses. I will not leave you or forsake you'" (Joshua 1:1, 5).

o "David led the troops and continued to be successful in all his activities because Yahweh was with him" (1 Samuel 18:13-14).

o Many, many other references could be cited, such as Daniel in the lions' den and Jonah in the whale.

The New Testament opens with the genealogy and birth of Jesus Christ. The first Old Testament quotation comes from Isaiah 7:14: "See, the virgin will become pregnant and give birth to a son, and they will name Him Immanuel, which is translated "God is with us."

John states in the first chapter of his gospel: "The Word became flesh and took up residence among us" (John 1:14). All four gospels reveal the fact of Yeshua continuously being present with His disciples.

The Acts and all remaining New Testament books focus on Yahweh's initiative in being with His people. Remember such experiences as His presence with Peter and Paul being held in prisons, and finally, the apostle John on the Isle of Patmos. **Yahweh is always with His people—Yahweh Shammah.**

Think about the visible reminders Yahweh has used to assure His people of His presence, such as the fire and the cloud over the tabernacle in the wilderness and the fact of the temple in Jerusalem. Then came that very significant Day of Pentecost described in Acts 2, when the infant church was baptized in Yahweh's Spirit. From that day on, **every believer has become the literal temple of God.** As Paul reminds us, "Don't you know that you are God's sanctuary and that the Spirit of God lives in you? (1 Corinthians 3:16). And again, "Do you not know that your body is a sanctuary of the Holy Spirit who is in you, whom you have from God? (1 Corinthians 6:19).

What an awesome truth! Yahweh is not only *with* us; He actually dwells *within* us! I do not know any fact that is more life altering than this one.

Yahweh's Powerful Presence

Now that we have considered the persistent nature of Yahweh's presence, let's move on to learn more about the effect of His Spirit living in us—what does this Divine Invader bring to us?

Jesus made a promise as He departed from His followers to return to heaven: "You will receive power when the Holy Spirit has come upon you, and you will be My witnesses in Jerusalem, in all Judea and Samaria, and to the ends of the earth" (Acts 1:8). The remainder of Acts is the remarkable story of what these first disciples were able to accomplish because of this new Power Source that filled them.

Think about the weaknesses of these apostles Jesus chose. These men were not the kind of prospects we would have chosen for the significant task of evangelizing the world. For the most part they were uneducated, inexperienced as teachers, and untrained to be leaders. Surely they were not the most promising recruits for the monumental challenge of giving strong capable guidance to the kingdom Jesus came to establish on earth.

And yet, these humble fishermen, along with other ordinary men, literally transformed history. How can this remarkable change be explained? Certainly not in terms of human achievement. Rather, by the power of divine enablement. As Jesus clearly promised, their ultimate and unfailing Power Source was the Holy Spirit who came to reside with them always.

Have you discovered this same life-changing power? Notice how Paul describes this amazing resource in his prayer for the Ephesian believers: "I pray that the God of our Lord Jesus Christ, the glorious Father, would give you a spirit of wisdom and revelation in the knowledge of Him. I pray that the eyes of your heart may be enlightened so you may know what is the hope of His calling, what are the glorious riches of His inheritance among the saints, and what is **the immeasurable greatness of His power to us who believe**, according to the working of His vast strength" (Ephesians 1:17-19).

Think further about this phrase, "the immeasurable greatness of His power to us who believe." We aren't dealing here with human strength or the power of a man-made resource. This gift is nothing less than the same power that created this universe, the power that keeps all creation functioning, and, as Paul goes on to say in this same passage, "He [Yahweh] demonstrated this power in the Messiah by raising Him from the dead and seating Him at His right hand in the heavens" (v. 20). **Resurrection power! Every believer has this "immeasurable greatness" residing in us—all the time!**

Remember the primary purpose for this power. As Jesus stated, "You will receive power . . . and you will be My witnesses" (Acts 1:8). Our foremost witness comes through a Christ-like life. In fact, unless we are living what we speak, our words will ring hollow and be ineffective. We must daily claim Yahweh's powerful presence to resist every attempt of Satan to deceive and lead us into sinful attitudes and behavior. These words, from an unknown author are on the wall of my study as an important reminder:

ATTITUDE

The longer I live, the more I realize the impact of attitude on life. Attitude, to me, is more important than facts. It is more important than the past, than education, than money, than circumstances, than failures, than successes, than what other people think or say or do. It is more important than appearance, giftedness or skill. It will make or break a company...a church...a home. The remarkable thing is we have a choice every day regarding the attitude we will embrace for that day. We cannot change our past...we cannot change the fact that people will act in a certain way. We cannot change the inevitable. The only thing we can do is play on the one string we have, and that is our attitude. I am convinced that life is ten percent what happens to us and ninety percent how we react to it. And so it is that we are in charge of our attitudes.

I must add to these words the fact that **we must trust the Holy Spirit for the power to make our attitude what it should be.** He alone can produce a consistent Christ-like attitude in us.

Being an effective witness goes beyond one's attitude and behavior. Unless we verbalize our witness, others will never discover the secret of a transformed life. Again, the Holy Spirit is the source of an effective spoken witness. The narrative of the Book of Acts repeatedly affirms this truth.

The word *bold* or *boldness* occurs nine times in the text of Acts. Each time the word refers to "speech that is clear, confident, and unhindered." Notice this first reference: "When they observed the **boldness** of Peter and John and realized that they were uneducated and untrained man, they were amazed and knew that they had been with Jesus" (Acts 4:13). Later in this same chapter we discover the kind of prayer these men offered that resulted in such boldness: "And now, Lord, consider their threats, and grant that Your slaves may speak Your message with complete **boldness**" (v. 29). And how was their prayer answered? "When they had prayed, the place where they were assembled was shaken, and they were all filled with the Holy Spirit and began to speak God's message with **boldness**" (v. 31).

Yahweh wants to loose our tongues to boldly speak truth about His saving grace. This truth doesn't mean we are to become brash or offensive in any way—just a quiet, clear, confident testimony to the good news of the transforming power of Yeshua. I encourage you to begin every day by offering your voice to speak His message with boldness. Why not use the same prayer of these early disciples: "Yahweh, grant that Your slave may speak Your message today with complete boldness." You will be amazed at what happens; hearers will know that you have been with Him, and His fellowship is what makes all the difference.

> *Yahweh wants to loose our tongues to boldly speak truth about His saving grace.*

Yahweh's Comforting Presence

Jesus knew that leaving His disciples would be a great loss for them. They depended entirely upon Him for everything about the new life they were experiencing. Therefore, He gave them assurance that His visible presence would be replaced by an invisible, spiritual companion, the one He referred to as the *Comforter.* He said, "I will ask the Father, and He will give you another Counselor [Comforter] to be with you forever. He is the Spirit of truth….He remains with you and will be in you" (John 14:16-17). Several other references are made to this special Comforter. (See John 14:25; 15:26; 16:6-14.)

The indwelling Spirit of God is with believers at all times. One of His ministries is to bring comfort to us. The word translated *Counselor* or *Comforter* literally means "one called alongside." The Holy Spirit comes alongside or inside us to be everything Jesus was to His disciples—and more. I say more because Jesus was not with His disciples every moment like the Holy Spirit is with us.

I want to share one of the most unusual personal experiences I can remember of how the Holy Spirit brings comfort in a time of distress. Several years ago I was traveling by plane from Nashville, Tennessee, to Sacramento, California. The plane landed in Dallas, Texas, to allow some passengers to deplane and others to board. Since I was continuing on the same flight, I remained in my assigned aisle seat.

After passengers got off the plane, the flight attendant made an unusual announcement. She told us that a group of Russian immigrants was coming on board. She said they did not speak English and asked our patience as they found their seats. The first to come down the aisle toward me was a man carrying a small child, leading another child by the hand, followed by his wife with two more children. The look on their faces was one of great anxiety.

While watching them, I remembered that my grandparents had come from Russia to American with their four children many years ago. Suddenly a feeling of compassion for these strangers came over me, a longing to be of help to them. How fearful they must be in this strange land, not knowing the language or the customs. The father put his bags in the luggage compartment above his seat and took his place just across from me. Two of his children were next to him. His wife and the other two children sat in the row of seats in front of him. I wanted to be of some assistance but due to the language barrier all I could do was offer a nod and smile to them.

Soon the plane took off and out of the corner of my eye I saw the father look at his wrist watch. When he turned on the compartment light above him to see the time more clearly, the time was wrong. So here was my chance to be of some help. Reaching my arm across the aisle I showed him the correct time on my watch. He smiled and nodded with a word that probably meant, "Thank you." He reset his watch and showed it to his wife seated in front of him.

As we settled back for the flight, there still was the desire to be of more help. Soon he took the magazine out of the seat pocket in front of him. I noticed that when he found the maps, he seemed to be looking at California. Here was another opportunity for me to assist, so I pointed on the map to Sacramento, and spoke that word to him. Again, he smiled and nodded to me. I felt so pleased to be of this kind of simple help.

Later I decided to do some Bible reading in preparation for the conference I was planning to lead. Unbuckling my seat belt, I stood up in the aisle, opened the luggage bin above me and found the brown, leather-covered Bible in my case. I then sat down, buckled up, pulled down the seat tray, opened my Bible, turned on the light and began reading.

My new neighbor was watching me. He must have assumed this is what all passengers were supposed to do at this time because he did exactly what I had just done. He stood up, opened the bin, found a brown leather-covered book in his bag, sat down, buckled up, pulled down the tray, turned on the light, and began reading. You can imagine my surprise to see this happen.

Being very curious, I looked to see what his book might be—probably some Communist propaganda I thought to myself. To my absolute amazement, I could tell by the way the pages were laid out that this man was reading a Russian Bible! Here's my chance to help this frightened man. So, I reached out and motioned for him to hand me his Bible, which he did. Although I could not read Russian, I was able to find Isaiah 41:10, by following the order of Bible books and reading the numbers, which were the same as English. I handed the Bible back to him with my finger on these words: **"Do not fear, for I am with you; do not be afraid, for I am**

your God. I will strengthen you; I will help you; I will hold on to you with My righteous right hand."

I watched closely as my new friend read these comforting words. He looked up with a new countenance, one of peace and of gratitude to me for this reminder. Then he found a passage in the Psalms, pointed to it as he gave his Bible back to me. Again, I located the same reference in my Bible, read other words of comfort and thanked him. He shared the Isaiah reading with his wife and she, too, seemed helped.

Soon we arrived at our destination. As we left the plane and entered the terminal, there was a large group of Russian-looking people waiting for these immigrants. They greeted them with hugs, kisses, and much joy. When I asked an air terminal employee standing nearby what was going on, he replied, "There's a settlement of Russian Baptists who live in this area; they are welcoming these family members and friends." Amazing!!

Watching this touching moment reminded me of the final home-going promised us in the New Jerusalem. Loved ones and friends who have preceded us will surely be there to welcome us. And according to Ezekiel, "the name of that city from that day on will be **Yahweh Shammah**" (Ezekiel 48:35).

Oh the comforting power of Yahweh's presence! What a help He is in our times of need. As I mentioned in chapter four, I want to strongly recommend that you memorize Isaiah 41:10 by letting each of your four fingers and thumb remind you of one of the five phrases from this encouraging promise. What a difference this will make! **The difference between our aloneness and His presence.**

Suggested prayer: **Gracious Yahweh Shammah, thank You for the assurance of Your abiding, unfailing presence every moment of every day. Thank You that although we may sometimes feel lonely, we are never alone; we never need to ask You to be with us. How grateful we are for the spiritual power You bring to us. Help us learn to claim this power for living Your kind of life, and for being bold in speaking our witness for You. How comforted we are in all times of distress, just knowing that You are present. All praise and honor be to Your sacred Name.**

Amen.

STUDY GUIDE

Chapter Eight: The Difference Between
Our Aloneness and His Presence

1. Why is the combination name *Yahweh Shammeh* so significant for us?

2. How would you describe Yahweh's Persistent Presence in your life? (Read 1 Corinthians 5:16 and 1 Corinthians 6:19.)

3. What difference does Yahweh's life-changing power make in you?

4. Describe a personal experience when the Holy Spirit has been your Comforter.

CHAPTER NINE

The Difference Between Separation From God and Intimacy with Him

YAHWEH ROHI
(YAH-way ROW-ee)

WHY IS THE 23ʳᴰ Psalm the favorite chapter of the Bible for many people? One reason is its familiarity. Think of how many times you have heard this chapter read at funerals and other special occasions. But another reason is its strong emphasis on a personal and intimate relationship between an individual and the Lord. In fact, this chapter has been called "The He-Me Psalm" due to the many personal pronouns, such as ". . . m*y* shepherd . . . *I* shall not want . . . *He* lets *me* lie down . . . *He* leads *me* . . . *He* renews *my* life . . .*He* leads *me* . . . *You* are with *my* . . . *Your* rod and *You*r staff—they comfort *me* . . . *You* prepare a table before *me* . . . *You* anoint *my* head . . . Only goodness and faithful love will pursue *me* all the days of *my* life, and *I* will dwell in the house of Yahweh as long as *I* live."

The psalmist David was boldly declaring the profound comfort he found in his intimate fellowship with Yahweh. He carefully described many of the benefits coming from this relationship that made a significant difference for him. We want to identify with this writer as we deal with life issues that are similar to his. The same assurance is desired that not only will all our present needs be met but we will ultimately "dwell in the house of Yahweh as long as I live." How can this confidence be ours?

What most readers do not know is that the Hebrew words for "The LORD is my shepherd" is one of the special combinations of Yahweh's name: *Yahweh Rohi.* One writer states: "No other divine title has the same tender, intimate touch as this." This is the kind of intimacy with Yahweh that most of us passionately desire; we want a strong, personal relationship with Him, not just information about Him. I keep these words from a praise song by Graham Kendrick taped to the inside cover of my Bible:

> Knowing You Jesus, knowing You
> There is no greater thing
> You're my all, You're the best,
> You're my joy, my righteousness
> And I love you Lord.
>
> Now my heart's desire is to know You more
> To be found in You, and be known as Yours
> To possess by faith, what I could not earn
> All surpassing gift of righteousness.

This meaningful prayer is a reminder of the focus that must be maintained if I am to become all Yahweh wants me to be. The good news is that such intimacy is available through *Yahweh Rohi.*

We must examine this special name more fully. The English word *shepherd* occurs about 80 times in the Bible. The Hebrew word is *rohi* and has various meanings, such as "feeder," "keeper," "companion," "friend," "pastor," and "shepherd." All these nouns describe the relationship between a shepherd and his sheep. He fed them, kept them from straying, and was their constant companion and friend, and cared for them. **Yahweh has given us the privilege of knowing Him as Yahweh Rohi so we can appreciate and experience all He wants to provide for us as our personal shepherd.**

I find much help in understanding Yahweh's role as our shepherd by learning from three modifying terms in the New Testament. These meaningful

Yahweh has given us the privilege of knowing Him as Yahweh Rohi so we can appreciate and experience all He wants to provide for us as our personal shepherd.

words refer to Him as "the Good Shepherd," "the Great Shepherd," and "the Chief Shepherd." Consider each of these terms.

The Good Shepherd

The 10th chapter of John records Yeshua's words about Himself as the Good Shepherd. He knew that His hearers were all very familiar with a shepherd's role in caring for sheep. He uses their understanding of a shepherd and his sheep to reveal what spiritual provisions He offers to all persons.

In this passage Jesus mentions three truths about Himself as the Good Shepherd. First, "I am the good shepherd. The good shepherd lays down his life for the sheep" (v. 11). Just as a shepherd would risk his life to protect his sheep from a wolf, Jesus declared that He had come to rescue sinners from Satan's destructive work by offering His life for their sake. This fact reveals the amazing love Yahweh has for all persons, however unworthy they may be. In His opinion all are worthy of His self-sacrificing love. **The Good Shepherd chose to die on a cross to save His sheep from perishing.**

The second truth is found in these words: "I am the Good Shepherd. I know My own sheep, and they know Me . . . My sheep hear My voice, I know them and they follow Me. I give them eternal life, and they will never perish—ever!" (vv. 14, 27-28). Here is a clear reference to the intimacy between the Good Shepherd and His sheep—He knows us and we know Him.

An interesting choice of words is found in this chapter. In verses 1-5 Jesus describes the true shepherd who comes to the door of the sheep pen and calls for his sheep to come out and follow him. Jesus said, "He calls his own sheep by name and . . . the sheep follow him because they recognize (know) his voice. They will not follow a stranger; instead they will run from him, because they don't recognize (know) the voice of strangers." The Greek word Jesus chose for "recognize" is often translated "know," as I have indicated in the above quote. This word means "to have knowledge of, to know from observation, to recognize."

However, when Jesus spoke later in this same chapter about His own sheep (followers), He chose a different word for "know." This term has the meaning of "understanding completely, referring to a relationship between the person knowing and the object known." (See vv. 14-15, 27.) **Thus when**

He spoke of knowing His sheep and His sheep knowing Him, He was intentionally referring to the intimate, personal relationship between Him and all who choose to follow Him as their Good Shepherd.

The third benefit of following Jesus as the Good Shepherd is found in these words: "I have come that they may have life and have it in abundance . . . . I give them eternal life, and they will never perish—ever!" (vv.10, 28). Notice that the new life He gives is abundant, eternal, and secure. What could be more *good* than that?

The Great Shepherd

The writer of the Book of Hebrews concluded his message with this benediction:

> "Now may the God of peace, who brought up from the dead our Lord Jesus—the great Shepherd of the sheep—with the blood of the ever-lasting covenant, equip you with all that is good to do His will, working in us what is pleasing in His sight, through Jesus Christ, to whom be glory forever and ever. Amen" (Hebrews 13:20-21).

The term "great Shepherd" appears here. Jesus spoke of the "good Shepherd" in terms of His crucifixion ("I lay down My life for the sheep."). Now we see the "great Shepherd" in relation to His resurrection ("brought up from the dead"). And when Yahweh brought Yeshua "up from the dead," He came "with the blood of the everlasting covenant"—His own blood from the cross. This means that all of the blood that was needed to provide atonement for all the sin of all the world has been offered and accepted by God.

Our part in this divine provision is to believe this promise, and by faith accept all that the great Shepherd offers us. The next step is more grace as Yahweh equips us "with all that is good to do His will, working in us what is well pleasing in His sight." The word used here for "equip" is very rich in meaning. It can be translated as "outfit a ship for a voyage" or "supply what soldiers need for a battle" or "restore and mend what has been broken or torn." In other words, **the Great Shepherd, by**

His Spirit, is now working in us to provide all we need to be and do everything that pleases God—His perfect will.

How exciting this fact is! **None of us will ever be lacking anything we need to do God's will.** And the One who supplies these needs is, Himself, at work in us to utilize all this provision. When we understand this amazing truth, and by faith claim it, we will never have to ask Yahweh God to give us more than we have—rather, we will thank Him for His abundant provisions and trust His power for doing His will.

> *None of us will ever be lacking anything we need to do God's will*

As I write these words I think of my grandson and his wife who are serving as missionaries to an unreached language group in an American metro area. (I would be more specific but their identity must be kept secret.) Although they are very young and inexperienced in this type of ministry, they are confident of Yahweh's provision of all they need to do all He has sent them to do. They believe He has equipped them for their task and that He is working in and through them to accomplish that task. This awareness gives them an amazing sense of peace and assurance that their labors are not in vain, in spite of the fact of very limited visible results. They are planting seeds that will eventually be brought to maturity and fruition.

How about your understanding of the difference the Great Shepherd wants to make in your service for Him? Have you learned the truths we have just considered from Hebrews? Let me urge you to give serious consideration and study to the amazing facts presented in the words of this benediction. Join me in memorizing these words and use them in your times of private worship as you thank Yahweh for His provision and presence. Also, offer this benediction as a prayer on behalf of others, just as I do for my grandson and his wife.

The Chief Shepherd

We are indebted to the apostle Peter for the single biblical occurrence of the term "chief Shepherd." As he came to the close of his first epistle, he wrote: "And when the chief Shepherd appears, you will receive the unfading crown of glory" (1 Peter 5:4). Warren Wiersbe is one of my favorite Bible interpreters. He says of this verse: "Jesus Christ is the *Good* Shepherd who died for the sheep (John 10:10), the *Great* Shepherd who lives for the sheep (Heb. 13:20-21), and the *Chief* Shepherd who comes for the sheep (1 Peter 5:4)."

Any group of shepherds in biblical times recognized one as the chief shepherd. He often gained that position as the result of age and experience, or due to his wealth. He might also be the one owning a large number of sheep and who paid other shepherds for their service. At the end of a shepherding season, these shepherds looked to the chief shepherd for their compensation.

In a similar manner, Peter wrote these words to the elders (leaders) of local churches who would read his epistle. He challenged them to "shepherd God's flock among you" (v. 2). Then to encourage them he promised that "when the chief Shepherd appears, you will receive the unfading crown of glory" (v. 4). Peter wrote this letter to give hope to believers who were suffering for their faith. He assured the local leaders (shepherds) that their labors would not go unrecognized nor be forgotten. The Chief Shepherd was coming back and would, at that time, fully reward them.

The word he chose for "crown" referred to the athlete's crown, often made of flowers and leaves. This recognition would quickly fade away. However, the Chief Shepherd would give "the unfading crown of glory." On the wall of my study are numerous framed expressions of appreciation from churches and other organizations that I have served. These reminders are places and people where I've had the privilege to minister as a shepherd. I am grateful for each of these plaques, but none of them compares to the eternal rewards awaiting every one of us who have served the Chief Shepherd.

I think of pastors and other leaders I have known who have given their entire ministries in serving in what the world would consider small and insignificant places. Their efforts have gone largely unnoticed and without public fanfare. Little recognition has come to them after years of faithful service. Sometimes these humble servants become discouraged and wonder if their work has been in vain.

For example, my son Mark and his wife Judy, have served as overseas missionaries for many years. First, they worked in Hong Kong, then Manila, Philippines, now in Singapore. Most of their efforts have been unnoticed by those outside their places of ministry. The people they helped were very limited in their ability to express gratitude in some tangible manner. **However, these faithful servants, like so many others, are encouraged by knowing their efforts to help the helpless are well known and remembered by Yeshua.** Speaking about the final judgment and the rewards He would distribute at that time, He said, "Come, you who are blessed by My Father, inherit the kingdom prepared for you from the foundation of the world . . . . I assure you: Whatever you did for one of the least of these brothers of Mine, you did for Me" (Matthew 25:34. 40). The writer of Proverbs expressed this same truth: "Kindness to the poor is a loan to Yahweh, and He will give a reward to the lender" (Proverbs 19:17).

Peter speaks to such loyal workers when he reminds them of a future day of recompense when every good deed will be fully rewarded. Hear these words from Jesus in the final chapter of the Bible: "Look! I am coming quickly, and My reward is with Me to repay each person according to what he has done" (Revelation 22:12). An old song, often sung by slaves, has these plaintive lines: "Sometimes I feel discouraged, and think my work's in vain. But then the Holy Spirit revives my soul again. There is a balm in Gilead to make the wounded whole. There is a balm in Gilead to heal the sin-sick soul."

Remember, the Chief Shepherd is coming back. And when He comes He will be faithful to fully reward every good work of every person who has been faithful to Him. What a difference this truth makes as we seek to honor Him day by day. Human applause and recognition are not needed. We are not motivated by earthly rewards. Rather, we look forward to His appearing for us or to our appearing before Him, whichever comes first.

The Shepherd's Psalm

This chapter began with a brief consideration of Psalm 23, the Shepherd's Psalm. David was the most likely writer. When we first meet him in the Bible, he is working as a shepherd boy, caring for his father's sheep (1 Samuel 16:11). Thus he knew from personal experience the intimate relationship between the shepherd and his sheep. Later when he became king, the people reminded him that Yahweh had said to him, "You will shepherd My people Israel and be ruler over Israel" (2 Samuel 5:2).

I want to conclude our study by examining this passage from a new perspective. I say "new" because even though we have heard and read this favorite chapter many times, the truths we have considered about Yahweh add a new dimension to our understanding and appreciation of these familiar words. (I am indebted to Dr. John Macbeth for pointing out these relationships between phrases of Psalm 23 and the combination names of Yahweh.)

Verse 1: "The LORD is my shepherd [*Yahweh Rhoi*]; there is nothing I lack [*Yahweh Yireh*]." You will recall that this name means "I AM the One who provides all you need."

Verse 2: "He lets me lie down in green pastures; He leads me beside quiet waters [*Yahweh Shalom*]." Here is a vivid picture of the peace and prosperity Yahweh gives.

Verse 3a: "He renews my life [*Yahweh Rophe*]." We all receive the spiritual healing and restoration that only He can supply.

Verse 3b: "He leads me along the right paths for His name's sake [*Yahweh Tsidkenu*]." Because He is righteous, He always leads us in the ways that are right.

Verse 4: "Even when I go through the darkest valley, I fear no danger, for You are with me: Your rod and Your staff—they comfort me [*Yahweh Shammah*]". The fact that Yahweh is always present makes the difference between panic and peace.

Verse 5: "You prepare a table before me in the presence of my enemies; You anoint my head with oil; my cup overflows [*Yahweh Nissi*]." These words give the picture of victory over all enemies; Yahweh's triumphant banner of victory waves over us as we enjoy His bountiful provisions in the presence of our enemies.

Verse 6: "Only goodness and faithful love will pursue me all the days of my life, and I will dwell in the house of Yahweh forever [*Yahweh*

M'kaddesh].” We are set apart as belonging to Yahweh from the moment of our entrance into His kingdom on earth, and throughout all eternity.

This psalm is such a beautiful picture of the intimate and complete care we receive from Yahweh Rohi. How comforting and reassuring!

And **so, we celebrate the revelation of God as Yahweh Rohi—I AM the SHEPHERD.** Here is a glorious truth that makes the difference between separation from God, which we all deserve, and a wonderful intimacy with Him.

Suggested prayer: **Faithful Yahweh Rohi, we rejoice in knowing You as our personal care-giver—our Shepherd. We know that we are all like sheep that go astray, and yet, You have come after us and brought us back to Your fold. Thank You for being the Good Shepherd who laid down Your life for us on the cross; thank You for being the Great Shepherd who arose from the dead to work in us Your perfect will; and thank You for being the Chief Shepherd who is coming again to receive us and reward us. All glory to You! Amen.**

STUDY GUIDE

Chapter Nine: The Difference Between Separation from God and Intimacy with Him

1. How do the words of Psalm 23 deliver us from fear of being separated from God?

2. What three truths are found in John 10 to reveal the spiritual provisions Yahweh Rophe offers?

3. Read again the benediction found in Hebrews 13:20-21. What difference can the Great Shepherd make in your service for Him?

4. What truth is found in 1 Peter 5:4 to encourage you to be faithfully serving the Chief Shepherd?

5. Search Psalm 23 as presented in the Shepherd Psalm subtitle section. List seven combination names of Yahweh from this psalm. How does each one express intimacy with God?

CHAPTER TEN

The Difference Between a Universe Controlled by Chance and One Controlled by YAHWEH

YAHWEH SABAOTH (TZAVA'OT)
(YAH-way tsa-ba-OAT)

EACH OF THE COMPOUND names we have studied is God's way of revealing truths about Himself. He wants us to know Him, and these expressions enable us to become better informed about His nature as well as to be better acquainted with Him. J.I. Packer wrote a very helpful book entitled *Knowing God.* Think about this quote from page 29 of his book:

"What were we made for? To know God. What aim should we set for ourselves in life? To know God. What is the 'eternal life' that Jesus gives? The knowledge of God. 'This is life eternal, that they might know thee, the only true God, and Jesus Christ, whom thou hast sent' (John 17:3). What is the best thing in life, bringing more joy, delight, and contentment, than anything else? Knowledge of God. 'This is what Yahweh says: "The wise must not boast in his wisdom; the mighty must not boast in his might; the rich must not boast in his riches. But the one who boasts should boast in this, that he understands and knows Me . . . ."' (Jeremiah 9:23-24). What does Yahweh desire from humankind? The knowledge of Himself. 'I desire . . . the knowledge of God more than burnt offerings: says God' (Hosea 6:6)."

Yes, we become better acquainted with God through these interesting name combinations. As Packer suggests, this understanding means we bring greater pleasure to God as well as more true wealth and prosperity to ourselves. **How exciting is this adventure of *growing in knowing*! How rewarding to contemplate the meaning of each revelation of the vast nature of Yahweh.** Consider next another very significant revelation of Him.

One Bible dictionary defines the sovereignty of God as "the biblical teaching that God is the source of all creation and that all things come from and depend upon Him. **Sovereignty means that God is in all and over all.**" The name *Yahweh Sabaoth* **expresses His sovereignty more clearly than any other.** As the psalmist declares, "The earth and everything in it, the world and its inhabitants, belong to Yahweh; for He laid its foundation on the seas and established it on the rivers . . . .Who is He, this King of glory? The LORD of Hosts [*Yahweh Sabaoth*], He is the King of glory" (Psalm 24:1, 10).

> *Sovereignty means that God is in all and over all." The name Yahweh Sabaoth expresses His sovereignty more clearly than any other.*

This compound name occurs over 285 times in the Old Testament and is quoted twice in the New Testament. The first occurrence in the Bible of **Yahweh Sabaoth** helps us understand what is revealed about Yahweh by this term. Let's begin by looking at the background of this initial reference. One of the most troublesome periods of Israel's history was that era (approximately 1380-1060 B.C.) when various judges ruled over them. Just prior to this time, Joshua had led God's people in the conquest of most of the Promised Land. God's people were at the height of their prosperity as they claimed this inheritance. But the Book of Joshua was followed by a period of decline, as Israel allowed the pagan influence of the Canaanites to lead them in the worship of various idols. This tragedy happened because God's people failed to follow His instructions to remove all the pagans and their idolatrous practices before moving into the land.

Thirteen various judges succeeded one another during a three hundred year period of highs and lows. Israel cycled between obeying God and turning from Him. A sad commentary is found in the closing verse of Judges: "In those days there was no king in Israel; everyone did whatever he wanted" (Judges 21:25).

Yahweh did not abandon His people, in spite of their unfaithfulness to Him. First Samuel is the story of the beginning of a new and improved era in Israel's history. This spiritual revival began with the birth of Samuel. He was God's chosen prophet, who would anoint Israel's first king, a man named Saul. The first episode in this interesting book is the account of Samuel's parents, Elkanah and Hannah. Elkanah made an annual pilgrimage to worship at Shiloh: "This man would take Hannah and go up from his town every year to worship and to sacrifice to the LORD of Hosts [**Yahweh Sabaoth**] at Shiloh" (1 Samuel 1:3).

Hannah was grieved because she could not give a child to her husband. One year she decided to make a vow: "Deeply hurt, Hannah prayed to the LORD and wept with many tears. Making a vow she pleaded, 'LORD of Hosts [**Yahweh Sabaoth**], if You will take notice of Your servant's affliction, remember and not forget me, and give Your servant a son, I will give him to the LORD all the days of his life, and his hair will never be cut" (1 Samuel 1:10-11).

Yahweh heard and honored this prayer. When her son was born, Hannah named him Samuel, meaning "requested from God." Here are the first biblical occurrences of **Yahweh Sabaoth.** As indicated in the text, *Sabaoth* literally means "hosts" or "multitudes." From other biblical references we understand these "hosts" to include all creation, such as angels (both holy angels and fallen angels), all humankind, all stars, planets, and solar systems, all plant life, animal life, sea creatures, birds—everything.

Thus since Elkanah and Hannah worshiped the ultimate sovereign ruler of the entire universe, Hannah felt confident He was able to supply her desire for a son. And He did! This trust is a good example for us to follow in our daily worship. We must focus our expressions of praise, gratitude, and submission to the One who is both creator and controller of all that exists, addressing Him as **Yahweh Sabaoth.**

Now let's look at various aspects of creation where Yahweh's sovereignty is revealed by Scripture. Each of these can enhance our worship as well as enlarge our awareness of His greatness—His omnipotence.

Sovereign Over All the Hosts of Creation

Consider the first time the word *sabaoth* ("hosts") occurs alone in the Bible: "So the heavens and the earth and all the **host** of them were finished" (Genesis 2:1). Here is a clear reference to all stars, planets, solar systems—

111

everything in "space." Yahweh planned, created, and controls all this vast, vast realm of the universe. The prophet Isaiah recorded these words from Yahweh: "'Who will you compare Me to or who is my equal?' asks the Holy One. Look up and see: who created these? He brings out the starry host by number; He calls all of them by name. Because of His great power and strength, not one of them is missing" (Isaiah 40:25-26).

You may be familiar with the Big Bang Theory endorsed by various cosmologists. This attempt to explain creation apart from intelligent design falls far short of the simple, but profound revelation of Scripture: "In the beginning God created the heavens and the earth" (Genesis 1:1). We who accept the authority of the Bible can readily agree with the writer of Hebrews who expressed his theory of creation in these familiar words: "By faith we understand that the universe was created by the word of God, so that what is seen has been made from things that are not visible" (Hebrews 1:3).

Scientists have made giant strides of progress in their ability to probe space. For example, the Hubble Space Telescope was launched from a space shuttle in 1990. This amazing device now orbits 353 miles above the earth sending hundreds of thousands of photos and other information back to earth. You may have seen the wondrous images of stars, galaxies, and planets coming from this technology—all confirming the glories of **Yahweh Sabaoth**.

The next planned development in this kind of stellar exploration is The James Webb Space Telescope to be launched in 2014, designed to orbit almost one million miles above the earth. This tennis-court-sized device will be stationed far beyond our moon, and will reveal even more of the wonders of God's creation.

When we attempt to grasp such vast regions of the creation, it "blows our mind." The most recent figure regarding the size of this universe is measured by "light years" (the distance light travels in one year at the speed of 186,000 miles per second). Observable matter (by telescope) is spread over a space of at least 93 billion light years in which there are over 100 billion galaxies with around 70 sextillion stars. Wow! Talk about big; this is far beyond our ability to even imagine.

And yet, **Yahweh created and controls all this universe**. I mention these facts in order to expand our knowledge and understanding of

Yahweh's greatness. As the psalmist so aptly stated: "The heavens declare the glory of God, and the sky proclaims the work of His hands. Day after day they pour out speech; night after night they communicate knowledge" (Psalm 19:1-2). Such truth should cause us, like this writer, to be filled with a sense of awe and amazement—to worship **Yahweh Sabaoth** with ever increasing praise and adoration.

Sovereign Over All the Hosts of Angels

One of the most fascinating and least understood subjects of biblical truth is that of the angels. How many sermons can you remember on the subject of angels? How often have you searched the scriptures to learn about these amazing creatures? And yet some form of the word *angel* occurs more than 300 times in the Bible and in 34 of its 66 books. Angels have played important roles in some of the most significant events of biblical history. Events such as the creation, God's communication to the patriarchs of the Old Testament, the outcome of various wars against Israel, the births of both John the Baptist and Jesus, announcement of Jesus' resurrection, explanation of His ascension and promised return, deliverance of the apostles from prison, and many happenings relative to the Second Coming of Christ and the final judgment. Seventy-seven references to angels are found in *Revelation,* more than in any other book of the Bible.

Surely we should pursue the quest for more information about such importance figures. I suggest you find books about angels, written from a biblical perspective. One of the most helpful I have found is *All the Angels of the Bible* by Herbert Lockyer, an older but very thorough study, written from a conservative perspective. I quote these words from this fine volume:

"The Bible assumes throughout that God is attended by a company or host of heavenly beings who are subordinate to Himself and who share His company and reflect His glory and majesty . . . . Angels are marvelous creatures, encompassed with splendor and glory; a God-given source of strength, inspiration, and encouragement to the faithful" (pp. 3, 9).

The terms *hosts* and *angels* often occur together as an indication of the multitude of these special servants of God. Notice this reference regarding the announcement to the shepherds of the birth of Jesus: "Suddenly there was a multitude of the heavenly host with the angel, praising God and saying: 'Glory to God in the highest heaven, and peace on earth to people He favors!' When the angels had left them and returned to heaven . . . ." (Luke 2:13-15).

The primary function of angels is to worship God and do whatever Yahweh bids them do. Often they serve as His special messengers. In fact in both Old and New Testaments, the root word for *angel* means "messenger." You also will notice that the term *evangelist* is built around "angel" and means "messenger of good news."

Another revelation regarding angels is their power to do battle. These "heavenly hosts" are often mentioned with reference to some type of warfare. But most often, angels appear as individuals who are sent on some special mission by Yahweh.

The belief that each Christian has a "guardian angel" assigned to protect and minister to them is based on passages such as these: "The angel of Yahweh encamps around those who fear Him, and rescues them" (Psalm 34:7), and "He will give His angels orders concerning you, to protect you in all your ways" (Psalm 91:11). In addition are many references to angels giving aid to various individuals in their times of need. The writer of Hebrews gives a good summary of the assignment of angels when he says, "Are they not all ministering spirits sent out to serve those who are going to inherit salvation?" (Hebrews 1:14).

Unfortunately, we find "fallen angels" mentioned in the Bible. Lucifer apparently was once a holy, ruling angel who rebelled against God, taking a large number of fellow angels with him. Thus we learn of the origin of Satan, demons, and evil spirits. In Revelation 12:7-9, this event is recorded: "Then war broke out in heaven; Michael and his angels fought against the dragon. The dragon and his angels also fought, but he could not prevail, and there was no place for them in heaven any longer. So the great dragon was thrown out—the ancient serpent, who is called the Devil and Satan, the one who deceived the whole world. He was thrown to earth and his angles with him."

Although we do not understand why this happened, we are given assurance that Yahweh and all His holy angels remain in ultimate control over all evil powers. We may be tempted and deceived by Satan, but can never be taken away by him from a personal and secure relationship with

God. The final destiny of Satan and his hosts is vividly described in this manner: "The Devil who deceived them was thrown into the lake of fire and sulfur where the beast and the false prophet are, and they will be tormented day and night forever and ever" (Revelation 20:10).

Yahweh Sabaoth's sovereign control over all the hosts of angels, both the good and the bad is revealed. We can be confident that He sends the holy messengers today to assist us in ways beyond our awareness.

Sovereign Over All the Earth and Its Inhabitants

The book of Daniel provides many examples of Yahweh's sovereignty. One very interesting expression of this supreme authority comes from Nebuchadnezzar, king of Babylon. After experiencing several demonstrations of Yahweh's amazing power, this pagan ruler declared, "His dominion is an everlasting dominion and His kingdom is from generation to generation. All the inhabitants of the earth are counted as nothing and He does what He wants with the army of heaven and the inhabitants of the earth. There is no one who can hold back His hand or say to Him, 'What have You done?'" (Daniel 4:34-35).

Nebuchadnezzar was including everything in heaven and on earth when he spoke of God's "dominion." This statement includes all kinds of animal life as well as humankind. For example, when Daniel was cast into the lions' den, he survived because, as he stated, "My God sent His angel and shut the lions' mouths" (Daniel 6:22). We can also point to another incident when God used a whale to transport His reluctant prophet Jonah. Or the time of famine when He fed Elijah by sending birds with food. "Yahweh said, 'I have commanded the ravens to provide for you'... and the ravens kept bringing him bread and meat in the morning and in the evening" (1Kings 17:4, 6).

Far more impressive is the testimony of the Bible regarding Yahweh's sovereignty over the affairs of all persons, nations, and armed forces. One very striking example comes from the reign of Hezekiah, king of Judah. The Assyrian army of 185,000 soldiers threatened to overcome Jerusalem and take the people into captivity. Hezekiah prayed to Yahweh, saying, "**Yahweh Sabaoth,** God of Israel, who is enthroned above the cherubim,

You are God—You –alone of all the kingdoms of the earth. You made the heavens and the earth. Save us from his hand so that all the kingdoms of the earth may know that You are Yahweh—You alone" (Isaiah 37:16, 20). His prayer was promptly answered when an angel came during the night and "struck down 185,000 in the camp of the Assyrians" (v. 30). Imagine that—one angel brought death to 185,000 strong soldiers in one night!

Now consider an example of a one-on-one battle where **Yahweh Sabaoth** revealed His might. You may recall the story of the contest between David, the shepherd boy, and Goliath, the Philistine giant. Goliath was nine feet and nine inches tall, and covered with armor that weighed 125 pounds. He challenged King Saul to send a warrior against him, with the agreement that the winner would have the opponent's entire army as servants. This challenge was repeated every morning and evening for 40 days.

When David visited his older brothers in the army of Israel, he heard this challenge and volunteered to go against the giant. King Saul reluctantly agreed to let David face Goliath. The giant mocked David and threatened to give his flesh to the vultures and wild beasts. Listen to David's reply, "You come against me with a dagger, spear, and sword, but I come against you in the name of **Yahweh Sabaoth**, the God of Israel's armies—you have defied Him. Today, Yahweh will hand you over to me . . . for the battle is Yahweh's. He will hand you over to us" (1 Samuel 17:45, 47). Sure enough, David used one stone and his sling to defeat mighty Goliath. **As you and I face personal "giants," we also must call upon Yahweh Sabaoth to exercise His sovereign authority and intercede on our behalf.** What a difference His name makes!

Many references to this special combination name are found throughout the writings of the Old Testament prophets. Perhaps the one with the most profound implications is given by Isaiah in these immortal words:

"For a child will be born for us, a son will be given to us, and the government will be on His shoulders. He will be named Wonderful Counselor, Mighty God, Eternal Father, Prince of Peace. The dominion will be vast, and its prosperity will never end. He will reign on the throne of David and over his kingdom, to establish and sustain it with justice and righteousness from now on and forever. The zeal of **Yahweh Sabaoth** will accomplish this" (Isaiah 9:6-7).

No one but Yahweh could ever bring to reality such an amazing prophecy. What a powerful testimony to His sovereignty over all history. And to think that He is now accomplishing these very happenings—all because of His love for us!

We find the Book of Malachi at the close of the Old Testament. His words were recorded over 400 years before the birth of Jesus Christ. In this brief document of four chapters, the name **Yahweh Sabaoth** occurs 23 times. God spoke strong words of warning and impending judgment through Malachi, but He included the promise of forgiveness and restoration. Listen closely to these words, noticing the references to *Yahweh Sabaoth*:

"'See, I am going to send My messenger, and he will clear the way before Me. Then the Lord you seek will suddenly come to His temple, the Messenger of the covenant you desire—see, He is coming,' says **Yahweh Sabaoth**" (Malachi 3:1). Here is a clear reference to the ministry of John the Baptist, followed by the first advent of Jesus Christ.

Malachi went on in these words to foretell the day of God's judgment on all the wicked: "'For indeed the day is coming, burning like a furnace, when all the arrogant and everyone who commits wickedness will become stubble. The coming day will consume them,' says **Yahweh Sabaoth,** 'not leaving them root or branches. But for you who fear My name, the sun of righteousness will rise with healing in its wings, and you will go out and playfully jump like calves from the stall. You will trample the wicked, for they will be ashes under the soles of your feet on the day I am preparing,' says **Yahweh Sabaoth**" (Malachi 4:1-3).

After more than four centuries of silence, John the Baptist made his appearance to "clear the way" for Jesus, "the Messenger of the covenant." Only **Yahweh Sabaoth** could have orchestrated these events and the timing of them to fulfill these amazing prophecies.

Earlier I spoke of two New Testament references to **Yahweh Sabaoth**. The first is found in these words of Isaiah, quoted by the apostle Paul: "If **Yahweh Sabaoth** had not left us a seed, we would have become like Sodom, and we would have been made like Gomorrah" (Romans 9:29). The second reference occurs when James warned the rich who had mistreated their hired workers: "Look! The pay that you withheld from the workers who reaped your fields cries out, and the outcry of the harvesters has reached the ears of **Yahweh Sabaoth**" (James 5:4). Both of these statements clearly reveal the difference made by the sovereignty of Yahweh. One Bible interpreter makes the very appropriate observation that **the name *Yahweh Sabaoth* refers to that "heavenly aid available to God's people in their time of need." This is God's name for man's extremity!**

> *the name Yahweh Sabaoth refers to that "heavenly aid available to God's people in their time of need." This is God's name for man's extremity!*

Psalm 46 is one of the best known and loved psalms. This comforting chapter begins with these words of assurance: "God is our refuge and strength, a helper who is always found in times of trouble." Then the statement: "**Yahweh Sabaoth** is with us; the God of Jacob is our stronghold" is found two times (vv. 7, 11). Why would the psalmist refer to Yahweh as the "God of Jacob"? Why not the God of Abraham or Moses or some other patriarch? One good reason is the fact that Jacob found himself in trouble more often than most others. Each time Jacob needed help, Yahweh showed up to help him—as this psalmist declared, "God is . . . a helper who is always found in times of trouble." The same God who was present many times to rescue Jacob, is available to us. And our Rescuer is none other than Yahweh Sabaoth—the One who is sovereign over all creation.

Martin Luther, the sixteenth century monk, was like Jacob in the sense of often finding himself in trouble. Perhaps this is why Psalm 46 was a favorite of his. He wrote a hymn in 1529, based on this psalm, which became known as "The Battle Hymn of the Reformation." As you read a portion of the text, notice the reference to "Lord Sabaoth His name."

> A mighty fortress is our God, a bulwark never failing;
> Our helper He amid the flood of mortal ills prevailing.
> For still our ancient foe doth seek to work us woe—
> His craft and power are great, and, armed with cruel hate,
> On earth is not his equal.

Did we in our own strength confide, our striving would be losing,
Were not the right man on our side, the man of God's own choosing,
Doest ask who that may be: Christ Jesus it is He—
Lord Sabaoth His name, from age to age the same,
And He must win the battle.

Just as Martin Luther discovered from his many trials—Yahweh Sabaoth is with us; "our helper He amid the flood of mortal ills prevailing." We can and must celebrate this fact.

As I write these words, I think of an impressive example of His presence in a time of extreme grief. Dennis and Berdena Sloan began attending the church where I was their pastor in Hobbs, New Mexico. He was a young police officer when she became the mother of their first child. One Sunday they went home after the morning worship service and as she was preparing lunch, this two-year old toddler went out the kitchen door into their garage. He found a small can of gasoline and was pouring it on his toy lawn mower. Soon the fumes reached the pilot light on the hot water heater, causing a terrible explosion.

I still remember that somber funeral service. We all stood as the parents walked to the front of the church and took their seats near the tiny casket. What impressed me most was the fact that Dennis was holding to his wife with one hand and carrying his Bible in the other. That book symbolized **Yahweh Sabaoth** to them. Through such promises as those found in Psalm 46, they found the courage and hope to endure this trial. What a difference He made!

Y.E.S.!

The first word for God in the Bible is the Hebrew term *Elohim* (e-lo-HEEM). "In the beginning God [Elohim] created the heavens and the earth" (Genesis 1:1). *Elohim* is actually a plural word but used as a singular noun—implying unity in plurality. In other words, God is a trinity of persons: Father, Son, and Holy Spirit, but He is one God. Although we cannot logically understand nor explain this mystery, we can accept it by faith and enjoy the blessings of the divine Trinity. Notice how this plurality is expressed in Genesis 1:26: "Then God (Elohim, plural) said,

'Let us (plural) create man in our (plural) image." All three persons of the Godhead were involved in the creation of humankind.

I mention the term *Elohim* **at this point in our study to focus our attention on a very special combination of words used to describe God**. The first occurrence of this combination is found in these words: "David became more and more powerful, and the LORD God of Hosts was with him" (2 Samuel 5:10). In the Hebrew language the three words "LORD God of Hosts" are: *Yahweh Elohim Sabaoth*. This combination occurs sixteen times in the Old Testament, and is the most awesome of all the biblical expressions of the sovereign power and authority of God. Look more closely at these words: *Yahweh* (the personal name of God, revealing Him as the covenant-making, covenant-keeping God), *Elohim* (the term to describe the all powerful triune creator of all there is), *Sabaoth* (a word that includes all the hosts of heaven and earth). **When these three words are blended into one combination name, they express the absolute, unequaled, sovereignty of God—infinitely supreme over all other powers and persons.**

Now examine the first occurrence of these three words. David, age 30, was just beginning his 40 years as king of Israel. One of his first acts was to organize an army and march against the Jebusites who occupied Jerusalem. They said to David, "You will never get in here. Even the blind and the lame can repel you" (2 Samuel 5:6). However, David actually overcame this mighty enemy. How was he able to conquer such a powerful adversary? Listen to this testimony: "David took up residence in the stronghold, which he named the city of David. He built it up all the way around from the supporting terraces inward. David became more and more powerful, and **Yahweh Elohim Sabaoth** was with him" (2 Samuel 5:9-10).

Those who opposed David and his army were, in fact, more powerful than they were. However, when **Yahweh Elohim Sabaoth** joined David's cause, the victory was easy. This same truth is repeated over and over in biblical events, as well as post-biblical history. What Paul wrote applies to us just as well as to his first readers: "...we are more than victorious through Him that loved us" (Romans 8:37). Remember, the One who is always with us is none other than **Yahweh Elohim Sabaoth**.

When I first became aware of this truth, I noticed that the first letters of these three Hebrew words spell YES, **Y**ahweh **E**lohim **S**abaoth. Since that simple discovery, I have made a practice of responding to every challenging situation with an affirmation of faith. Can I do what God calls me to do? **YES**. Am I able to be all He wants me to be? **YES**. Is there hope in this discouraging situation? **YES**. Will God use me to make a difference for others? **YES**. All these statements of assurance are based, not on me and my abilities, but on the One who is forever with me to make me strong and adequate for whatever comes—**Yahweh Elohim Sabaoth, the God of the eternal YES!! What a difference a name makes!**

Suggested prayer: **Most sovereign Yahweh Sabaoth. You are supreme in power and authority over all creation. We bow before You with a sense of heartfelt awe and wonder. How great You are! And how amazing that You have chosen us to be in Your family. We claim Your promise to inhabit us and to work Your will in and through us.**

Our desire is that You will be known through the witness of our daily walk. May we so reveal Your character that others will be attracted to You and discover who You are. Thank You for revealing Yourself through these special terms. Teach us to appropriate all You want to be for us and in us. We find pleasure in knowing that we can be and do all that pleases You because You are Yahweh Elohim Sabaoth, now and forever. Amen.

STUDY GUIDE

Chapter Ten: The Difference Between a Universe Controlled by Chance and One Controlled by Yahweh

1. Define in your own words the meaning of the sovereignty of God.

   (Compare your definition to the one in the fourth paragraph of this chapter.)

2. Three realms of Yahweh's sovereignty are discussed in this chapter. Which one is most impressive to you? Why?

3. Where is the term *Yahweh Elohim Sabaoth* first found in the Bible? How many total occurrences of the term are there?

4. Identify a personal challenge where Y.E.S. (*Yahweh Elohim Sabaoth*) can make a difference.

CHAPTER ELEVEN

The Difference Between Our Despair and His Hope

ADONAI YAHWEH
(a-doe-NAI YAH-way)

PERHAPS THE SINGLE MOST traumatic condition for any person is to be without hope. We sometimes refer to this as despair—a word meaning "to be without hope." Such desperation can result in extreme depression or even suicide. **Most of us can recall times in our past when a situation seemed hopeless to us.** We felt helpless to improve our outlook for the future. You may even be dealing with some of these feelings now.

My cousin Mike Laufer and his wife Faye serve as volunteer missionaries in Athens, Greece, where they minister to refugees from the Middle East. These persons have been forced to leave their homelands and seek asylum in another country. We can only imagine how devastated they feel as they consider the bleakness of their outlook for the future. The day they will be allowed to return to their homes may never come. They are literally homeless, separated from all that gave them a sense of belonging and security.

Mike and Faye have joined other volunteers who seek to build relationships of love and trust through acts of generosity and kindness. They distribute clothing and food, provide shelter and means of sanitation to these desperate strangers. Each day an invitation is extended to them for Bible study, prayer, and language study. Although the response seems very slow, several of these refugees have come to faith in Christ and agreed to be baptized.

This story about my cousin may seem rather irrelevant to us; we certainly are not like these homeless people. And yet, **sometimes a sense of hopelessness comes to individuals who seem to have everything materially.** What about the hope for improved health, or a better marriage, or restored relationships? What about senior adults who may have lost the sense of significance that comes from meaningful careers? The list could go on of situations where hope seems illusive.

My point in making these references is to magnify the appeal of the hope offered by Yahweh to everyone, regardless of their circumstances. We discover such hope by a study of God's Word, the Bible. Listen to these words from the apostle Paul as he speaks of the value of the Old Testament writings: "For whatever was written before was written for our instruction, so that through the endurance and through the encouragement of the Scriptures we may have hope....Now may the God of Hope fill you with all joy and peace in believing, so that you may overflow with hope by the power of the Holy Spirit" (Romans 15:4, 13). Notice the references to the Word of hope, the God of hope, and the Spirit of hope. These terms are the sources of hope we so desperately need.

The Combination of Adonai Yahweh

In this chapter we will go to the Word of hope to consider another Yahweh combination, one that relates directly to our need for hope—**_Adonai Yahweh_**. The word *adonai*, like *elohim*, is a plural Hebrew noun. This term is most interesting because *adon,* the singular form, is used when referring to a man, while the plural *adonai* is used when referring to God. Again, the fact of God's plural or trinitarian nature is expressed. *Adonai* is translated "Lord" in our English Bibles, and means master, ruler, sovereign one, or owner. Some 340 occurrences of this important word are found in the Old Testament.

You will recall that *Yahweh Sabaoth* is a strong expression of God's absolute sovereignty. **_Adonai Yahweh_** also declares His sovereignty, with this distinction: The first term, *Yahweh Sabaoth*, is more general in nature. That is, Yahweh is sovereign over all creation regardless of humankind's response. In other words, Yahweh has created all there is, and controls all there is, whether we acknowledge this fact or not. **_Adonai Yahweh_**

is a more personal reality. We become involved with His ownership by submitting to Jesus Christ as our own Master, Owner, and Lord. This truth will be the emphasis in the present chapter.

Translating this combination, ***Adonai Yahweh***, creates an interesting challenge for Bible scholars. Most translations render Adonai as "Lord" (lower case) and Yahweh as "LORD" (upper case). Thus when these occur together, the translation should read "Lord LORD." But since this repetition looks confusing, translators most often have chosen to render this term as "Lord GOD." So when you read "Lord GOD," the actual words are ***Adonai Yahweh***. Here is another example of how the use of some other word for *Yahweh,* in this instance "GOD," actually misleads the reader and fails to convey the actual meaning.

There also are several references where *LORD* (Yahweh) and *Lord* (Adonai) occur in the same verse. For example, in Psalm 16:2, we read: "I said to the LORD, 'You are my Lord; I have no good beside You'" Also, this quote from Psalm 110:1, "The LORD declared to my Lord: 'Sit at My right hand until I make Your enemies Your footstool.'" **Unless you are informed about the differences in the use of this one English term, *Lord*, you will miss the significance of these references.**

The first occurrence of these two words as a combination is in Genesis 15. This chapter is very significant because it reveals to us the covenant that God made with Abram (vv. 18-19). Since the covenant had to do with Abram's descendants, he was concerned because he and Sarah had no son to be their heir. Abram said to Yahweh, "Lord GOD (**Adonai Yahweh**) what can You give me, since I am childless and the heir of my house is Eliezar of Damascus" (15:2). Yahweh responded with the promise of a son through whom Abram's descendents would eventually become as numerous as the stars, and also would possess the land He had promised.

Abram believed Yahweh, but went on to ask, "Lord GOD (**Adonai Yahweh**) how can I know that I will possess it?" (v.8). God proceeded to confirm His promise by a covenant ceremony. Notice that Abram referred two times to God as "**Adonai Yahweh**," and this instance is the first such reference in the Bible. Why did Abram choose this expression at this time in his history? Why did he deliberately place these terms together on this occasion? I believe he wanted to affirm the fact that Yahweh was the One who owned him and was thus his master and lord—the One who had called him to leave his original home and travel a long distance to this place of promise. Abram came because the call and promise of Yahweh gave him hope—the hope of a significant future. This hope rested on the faithfulness of Yahweh who was Abram's master, lord, and owner.

Yahweh's Special Treasure

Several years ago, I was interested to discover that God has a "special treasure." The first mention of this treasure is found in Exodus 19. Moses has just led the Israelites out of Egypt and into the wilderness. While they were encamped near Mount Sinai, God called Moses up the mountain where He spoke these memorable words, "If you will indeed obey My voice and keep My covenant, then You shall be **a special treasure** to Me above all people; for all the earth is Mine. And you shall be to Me a kingdom of priests and a holy nation" (vv. 5-6 NKJV). The Hebrew word for "special treasure" is *segullah,* a word that occurs just eight times in the Old Testament. (See previous reference to *segullah* in Chapter 5.)

Consider another of these interesting references: "You are a holy people to Yahweh your God; Yahweh, your God has chosen you to be a people for Himself, **a special treasure** above all the peoples on the face of the earth .... Yahweh has brought you out with a mighty hand, and redeemed you from the house of bondage, from the hand of Pharaoh king of Egypt" (Deuteronomy 7:6, 8 NKJV).

One final quotation found in the last book of the Old Testament is especially interesting. Yahweh says of His people, "'They will be mine,' says the LORD of Hosts (Yahweh Sabaoth), '**a special possession** (segullah) on the day I am preparing'" (Malachi 3:17). Each of these statements clearly affirms the fact that from among all the peoples of the earth Yahweh has chosen some to be His **special treasure**—His prized possession.

Israel was this segullah in Old Testament times. Who are the ones who comprise this treasure today? We are indebted to the apostle Peter for the answer to this important question. In his first epistle, written to all who know Jesus Christ as Savior and Lord, he applied these words from the prophets to them: "You are a chosen race, a royal priesthood, a holy nation, **a people for His possession,** so that you may proclaim the praises of the One who called you out of darkness into His marvelous light. Once you were not a people, but now you are God's people; you had not received mercy, by now you have received mercy" (1 Peter 2:9-10).

All Christians are God's special treasure, His segullah. He claims complete ownership of us. Every person who has turned from sin to welcome, by faith, Jesus Christ as Lord can identify with the Israelites. We literally belong to the Lord Jesus Christ; He is our owner. Paul wrote of this amazing truth in these words: ". . . you are not your own, for you were bought at a price; therefore glorify God in your body and in your spirit, which are God's" (1 Corinthians 6:20 NKJV). Since we belong to Him, we can count on Him to provide for our every need. This truth is the firm basis for a future that is secure in every way.

Paul's reference to our being "bought at a price" came from the slave markets of his day. Slaves were auctioned much like cattle auctions today. Potential owners bought slaves by offering the highest price. In like manner, Jesus died on a cross to pay the price required to set us free from enslavement to sin. Having paid that enormous price, He now owns us; we are His redeemed possessions. Therefore, we have a hope that is eternally secure.

Jesus Christ as Lord

The Greek word for *Lord* is "kurios" which occurs about 650 times in the New Testament; the basic meaning is that of authority because of ownership. The truth that Jesus Christ is Lord is affirmed by passages such as Peter's sermon on the Day of Pentecost, when he boldly declared: "Let all the house of Israel know with certainty that God has made this Jesus whom you crucified both Lord and Messiah" (Acts 2:36). Paul's letter to the believers in Philippi contains these words: "God also highly exalted Him and gave Him the name that is above every name, so that at the name of Jesus every knee should bow—of those who are in heaven and on earth and under the earth—and every tongue should confess that Jesus Christ is Lord, to the glory of God the Father" (Philippians 2:9-11).

These Scriptures declare that what the Old Testament reveals about *Adonai Yahweh*, finds its fulfillment in the Lord Jesus Christ; He is the ultimate revelation of Adonai Yahweh. We who know Him as Savior, also belong to Him as our personal Lord and Master. However, in order for His lordship to be actual, we must choose to submit ourselves to

His control; we must become obedient to His commands. On one occasion Jesus said to His disciples, "Why do you call Me 'Lord, Lord,' and don't do the things I say?" (Luke 6:46). Many commands of Jesus could be considered here. Focus your attention on one of the first and most basic commands for every follower of Jesus.

We will consider what He said about two crosses. First, the cross on which Jesus died. He spoke of this cross when He told His disciples, "The Son of Man must suffer many things and be rejected by the elders, chief priests, and scribes, be killed, and be raised the third day" (Luke 9:21). He immediately referred to a second cross as He went on to say, "If anyone wants to come with Me, he must deny himself, take up his cross daily, and follow Me" (Luke 9:22). The word He used for "deny himself" means to disregard one's own self interests—to say no to self centeredness. This action is more than denying oneself certain pleasures; for this reason Jesus added "take up his cross daily." A cross is a place to die! Jesus' cross meant death for Him; our cross means death for us—not physical death, but death to self.

The apostle Paul described this death in these interesting words: "I have been crucified with Christ; and I no longer live, but Christ lives in me. The life I now live in the flesh, I live by faith in the Son of God, who loved me and gave Himself for me" (Galatians 2:19-20). Here is a good example of what it means to deny oneself and take up one's cross. A person chooses to consider his old self-centered life to be dead—crucified with Christ, and his new life to be the very life of Christ. Such a step requires faith, the faith to believe that such a personal, spiritual death and resurrection is possible.

Sometimes we hear a person speak of a particular trial they are experiencing as being their cross. They may say, "Well, this difficulty is just my cross and I will have to bear it." But when Jesus spoke of our cross, He wasn't referring to some unwanted trial that is thrust upon us—something we are forced to endure. Rather, our cross involves something we choose; we choose to die to our self. **If Jesus is to be our Lord, we must decide to say no to ourselves, die to our self-centeredness, and submit to Him as the One in charge of our lives.** And, He said that we must do this "daily."

> If Jesus is to be our Lord, we must decide to say no to ourselves, die to our self-centeredness, and submit to Him as the One in charge of our lives.

Another way of understanding the meaning of complete submission to Jesus as Lord is found in the term "filled with the Holy Spirit." In the Book of Acts we are given numerous references to various persons being filled with the Holy Spirit. This phrase does not refer to being filled in the same sense of a vessel being filled with some liquid. Rather, the meaning is that of being *controlled* by the Holy Spirit. Just as a person being filled with fear is controlled by fear.

One question is often asked regarding being filled with the Holy Spirit: **How do I know when I am Spirit-filled?** Will I speak in some new language like those disciples did on the Day of Pentecost? Or will I be able to perform miracles such as others did in the book of Acts? How can I know if the Holy Spirit is controlling me? I believe the best answer to this question is found in Paul's letter to the believers in the churches of Galatia. He described the old self-controlled life as the "works of the flesh" (Galatians 5:19). He then listed about 15 expressions of this old sinful lifestyle.

Next he spoke of the new, Holy Spirit controlled behavior as demonstrating the "fruit of the Spirit." Notice these nine qualities produced by the Spirit: "love, joy, peace, patience, kindness, goodness, faith, gentleness, self-control" (vv. 22-23). These descriptions are not nine separate "fruits" of the Spirit, rather they are nine aspects of one "fruit of the Spirit." In other words, **when we yield ourselves to His control, the Holy Spirit produces a Christ-like behavior in us.** Our attitude, character, and conduct reflect these nine qualities. Such qualities are the best evidence of a Holy Spirit filled person.

One example of being filled with the Holy Spirit is seen in a man named Barnabas, whose name means Son of Encouragement. He is described as "a good man, full of the Holy Spirit and of faith." (Acts 11:24). Wherever Barnabas appears in Acts, he is involved in some kind of helpful ministry. He found great pleasure in giving encouragement to others. He was truly a selfless person. We never find him feeling sorry for himself or seeking to gain some favor from others. He had died to himself and was alive in Christ and for Christ. Barnabas was allowing the Holy Spirit to control him—daily. What a clear example of the meaning of denying oneself, taking up a cross, and following Jesus.

This kind of commitment does not imply that a person must abandon his family, vocation, and every connection to this world. Rather, **the**

Spirit-filled person becomes a servant to his or her family, serves the Lord through a vocation (of His choice), and seeks to make a positive difference in every relationship. The freedom to adopt such a selfless lifestyle comes as the result of knowing Jesus as Lord—He is one's owner and Master; He promises to provide for every need and guide in every important decision. Such assurance provides the confidence—the hope, that all disciples of Jesus can embrace by faith.

What a difference such security makes! We no longer have to "make things happen," no longer are we responsible to "make ourselves successful." He takes over the management of our lives and we are freed from the fear and stress of seeking to manipulate our way to achieve self gratifying goals for ourselves.

Suggested prayer: **Adonai Yahweh, thank You for revealing Yourself to us as our Lord, Master, and Owner. Thank You for paying the price to purchase our freedom, and to deliver us from the bondage of sin. I claim Your help as I seek to present myself to Your control throughout every day. May You manifest Your own beautiful life through my words and behavior. I affirm that I am crucified with You and live only because of Your life in me. I bless you for filling me with joy, peace, and hope. Amen.**

STUDY GUIDE

Chapter 11: The Difference Between Our Despair and His Hope

1. What is the meaning of being in a hopeless situation?

2. Explain the biblical difference in the meaning of *LORD* and *Lord*.

3. How are you given hope by the awareness that you are Yahweh's *segullah?*

4. How would you correct this statement: "This difficulty is just my cross and I have to bear it."?

5. What does being filled with the Spirit have to do with hope?

CHAPTER TWELVE

The Difference Between Salvation and Condemnation

YESHUA
(ya-SHU-ah)

S UPPOSE YOU WERE ASKED to express in one word your greatest personal need. How would you respond? You might consider words such as peace, or hope, or health or even money. Whatever need seems the most pressing at the moment would probably determine your answer. But if you agree with God's Word, you would choose the term *salvation.* **Every person needs salvation more than anything else.** Why is this statement true?

Consider these words from the Holman Bible Dictionary: "The biblical idea of salvation involves three notions. First, is the rescue from danger, harm, or even death of an individual, group, or nation. More specifically salvation is the rescue from sin and death. Second is the renewing of the spirit. . . .God's salvation always renews the spirit of a person to lead a life that is morally pleasing to Him. Third is the restoration of a right relationship with God . . . . In both the Old and New Testaments God's salvation includes rescue, renewal, and restoration and is accomplished through the person and work of His Son, our Lord and Savior Jesus Christ" (page 1434).

More than any other need, however urgent, is our spiritual need to be rescued from perishing, made new by the miracle of regeneration and restored to a right relationship with Yahweh. All these personal needs are included in the biblical concept of salvation. How comforting to know that Yahweh is often described as "God of my salvation" (Psalm 88:1). His ultimate purpose for all humankind is to accomplish the rescue, renewal, and restoration so desperately needed. "Our God is a God of salvation, and escape from death belongs to Adonai Yahweh" (Psalm 68: 20).

The fulfillment of Yahweh's salvation plan is found in a person. Before Jesus was born an angel appeared to a man named Joseph informing him that Mary, to whom he was engaged to be married, would give birth to a very unique son. This child would be conceived, not by Joseph, but by the Holy Spirit. The angel said, "She will give birth to a son, and you are to name Him Jesus, because He will save His people from their sins" (Matthew 1:21). Of all possible names for His Son, why would Yahweh choose this particular name and insist that Joseph use it? *Jesus* **is the Greek form of the Hebrew name** *Joshua* **(Yeshua) which means "Yahweh saves."** Every time the name *Jesus* (**Yeshua**) appears in the New Testament (more than 700 times), the Bible is declaring the fact that our greatest need—salvation—is available through Him!

Many references in Scripture identify Jesus with salvation. When Mary and Joseph took Jesus to the temple in Jerusalem, an elderly man named Simeon was present. The Holy Spirit had informed him that he would not die until he saw "Yahweh's Messiah." Simeon took the infant Jesus in his arms and said, "Now, Master, You can dismiss Your slave in peace, according to Your word, for **my eyes have seen Your salvation**" (Luke 2: 25-29).

Paul wrote these memorable words to young Timothy, "This saying is trustworthy and deserving of full acceptance: '**Christ Jesus came into the world to save sinners**'—and I am the worst of them" (1 Timothy 1:15). The writer of Hebrews declared, "Though a Son, He learned obedience through what He suffered. After He was perfected, **He became the source of eternal salvation to all who obey Him**" (Hebrews 5:8-9). And, "**He is always able to save those who come to God through Him,** since He always lives to intercede for them" (Hebrews 7:25).

Unfortunately, there are many religious leaders today who acknowledge Jesus as a Savior, but go on to affirm other ways of salvation. They maintain that a person can be saved through various religions or attempts to reach God as long as they are sincere in what they believe. What does the Bible say? Listen to these words from Peter, "There is salvation in no one else, for there is no other name under heaven given to people by which we must be saved" (Acts 4:12). John wrote, "And this is the testimony: God has given us eternal life, and this life is in His Son. The one who has the Son has life. The one who doesn't have the Son of God does not have life" (1John 5:11-12). Finally, Jesus said of Himself, "I am the way, the truth, and the life. No one comes to the Father except through Me" (John 14:6). **Yeshua is more than one means to salvation; He is the ONLY SALVATION!**

The I AM of Salvation

Bible students are indebted to John, the apostle of Jesus, for his diligence to include significant sayings of Jesus, not recorded elsewhere in Scripture. *The Gospel of John* and the *Revelation* are the only books of the Bible where these expressions are found. I am referring to the various "I AM" statements of Jesus. As presented earlier in this book, *Yahweh* means "I AM." Therefore Jesus' name in Hebrew—**Yeshua**, a combination of *Ye* (shortened form of Yahweh) and *shua* (salvation)—reveals a connection between His I AM statements and His provision of salvation. We will point these relationships out as we examine each occurrence.

Notice these statements where just the words I AM are given by Jesus. The first instance was when Jesus spoke to the woman at the well in Samaria. She said, "I know that Messiah is coming. When He comes, He will explain everything to us." Jesus replied, "**I AM**, the One speaking to you" (John 4:25-26). Then recall the time the disciples were caught by a storm at night on the Sea of Galilee. Suddenly they saw Jesus approaching them, walking on the sea. He said to them, "**I AM**. Don't be afraid" (John 6:20). Later He spoke these solemn words as a warning to His listeners, "If you do not believe that **I AM**, you will die in your sins" (John 8:24). This same audience heard Him say, "When you lift up the Son of Man, then you will know that **I AM** . . . . Before Abraham was **I AM**" (vv. 28, 58).

Only John tells about Jesus washing the disciples' feet at the last supper. Following this episode Jesus warned that one of them would betray Him. He then said, "I am telling you now before it happens, so that when it does happen you will believe that **I AM**" (John 13:19). The final occurrences were all within a brief conversation Jesus had with those enemies who came to arrest Him, just before His crucifixion. When the soldiers, led by Judas, came to the garden of Gethsemane, they approached Jesus. He asked, "Who is it you're looking for?" They replied, "Jesus the Nazarene." Jesus told them, "**I AM.**" Upon hearing this and experiencing what must have been a supernatural revelation of His glory, they all "stepped back and fell to the ground" (John 18:36). How amazing that this body of armed soldiers would all be swept off their feet when confronted by the presence of the holy, Son of God! What awesome power! Now consider the following expressions of **I AM** in conjunction with various metaphors.

I AM the bread of life.

Only one miracle of Jesus is recorded in all four gospels—His feeding of 5,000 persons from a few fish and loaves of bread. John relates this event in Chapter 6 of his gospel. The day following this miracle, the same crowd found Jesus on the opposite side of the Sea of Galilee. He accused them of searching for Him because they wanted more food. He said, "Don't work for the food that perishes but for the food that lasts for eternal life, which the Son of Man will give you, because God the Father has set His seal of approval on Him" (John 6:27). Just as food is essential to our physical bodies, the Bread of Life is absolutely necessary for our spiritual life and health. Yeshua is the only source of this kind of nourishment.

Chapter 6 of John's gospel reveals more about the Bread of Life than any other portion of Scripture. Jesus refers to Himself as bread eleven times in this passage. The focus of His words was clear and simple: "I am the living bread that came down from heaven. If anyone eats of this bread he will live forever. The bread that I will give for the life of the world is My flesh" (6:51). Yeshua was referring to salvation. He came to offer His body ("flesh") as a sacrifice for every person's sin. All who choose to believe in Him and, by faith, receive Him, receive eternal life.

Notice His repeated emphasis on *eating and drinking* His flesh and blood. Several times He declared, "Unless you eat the flesh of the Son of Man and drink His blood, you do not have life in yourselves" (vv. 53-57). These statements seem, on the surface, to advocate cannibalism. However, Jesus went on to say, "The words that I have spoken to you are spirit and are life" (v. 63). His point was that just **as surely as an individual must**

actually partake of food by eating and drinking it, so believers must partake of Him, receive Him by faith.

The Lord's Supper is a graphic portrayal of all Jesus intended by referring to eating and drinking His body and blood. The broken bread of the supper symbolizes His body, broken on the cross. The content of the cup represents His poured-out blood. How significant that we are not commanded simply to look upon these symbols and remember His sacrifice. Rather we are told to *eat* the bread and *drink* from the cup. Such participation in this memorial supper expresses our belief that **salvation results from a personal relationship with the One who is the Bread of Life.**

I AM the light of the world.

God's first words in Genesis are: "Let there be light" (Genesis 1:3). He was referring both to physical light, such as from the sun, and also the light of truth. The prologue of John's gospel gives further information on this vital subject by stating, "In the beginning was the Word [Yeshua], and the Word was with God, and the Word was God . . . . Life was in Him and that life was the light of men. That light shines in the darkness, yet the darkness did not overcome it" (John 1:1-5).

The Bible uses the term *darkness* to refer to that which is false, evil, sinful, ignorance, and spiritual blindness. *Light*, on the other hand, expresses truth, goodness, and understanding. This basic difference is clearly seen the first time **Yeshua** made this bold claim: "I am the light of the world. Anyone who follows Me will never walk in the darkness but will have the light of life" (John 8:12). A woman had been caught in the act of adultery and was sentenced by the Jewish religious leaders to be stoned to death. When **Yeshua** was asked His opinion regarding her punishment, He wisely replied, "The one without sin among you should be the first to throw a stone at her" (v. 7). Upon hearing these words, the men slowly walked away. This woman was saved from an unjust execution due to the light of Jesus' words. He spoke a truth that opened the eyes of her accusers, causing them to cease their evil plan.

Yeshua came to save everyone from the darkness of ignorance and sin. He said, "I have come as a light into the world, so that everyone who believes in Me would not remain in darkness" (John 12:46). His words and His life reveal truth, the truth about God and the life God wants for everyone. The psalmist affirmed this fact when he wrote, "Yahweh is my light and my salvation—whom should I fear?" (Psalm 27:1). Think of how totally ignorant we would be concerning the nature of God if Jesus had not come to make Him known. As He said to His disciples, "The one who has seen Me has seen the Father" (John 14:9).

Imagine what your life would be like if you were physically blind. You would be totally dependent on others for knowledge about your surroundings. In a similar way, **sin blinds us so that we cannot perceive the truth about ourselves and about God.** We will remain in such darkness unless someone comes to our aid. How fortunate we are that **Yeshua** has come to rescue us! As one of our favorite hymns states: "I once was lost but now am found, was blind but now I see." Celebrating this saving grace is one aspect of worship.

But how can the Light of the World be seen now that He is in heaven? How can those in darkness be helped? A twofold answer to these questions is given. First, the light of His Word continues to reveal truth as the Bible is read and taught. As the psalmist declared, "Your word is a lamp for my feet and a light on my path . . . . The revelation of Your words brings light and gives understanding to the inexperienced" (Psalm 119: 105, 130).

Second, **we who have received Him become conveyors of the light of His Life**. Jesus gave a huge responsibility to all His followers when He said, "You are the light of the world . . . . let your light shine before men, so that they may see your good works and give glory to your Father in heaven" (Matthew 5:14, 16). Paul added to this task when he wrote: ". . . the god of this age has blinded the minds of the unbelievers so they cannot see the light of the gospel of the glory of Christ, who is the image of God . . . for God, who said, 'Light shall shine out of darkness'—He has shone in our hearts to give the light of the knowledge of God's glory in the face of Jesus Christ" (2 Corinthians 4:4, 6). Ponder this solemn truth: **We who have received Yeshua are like lamps that shine forth His glorious light to those in darkness.** Wow, what a privilege! What a responsibility!

Graham Kendrick has captured this awesome reality in his song, "Shine, Jesus Shine."

As we gaze on Your kingly brightness
So our faces display Your likeness,
Ever changing from glory to glory;
Mirrored here, may our lives tell Your story;
Shine on me, shine on me.

I AM the door.

Several I AM statements of Jesus were the result of His involvement with some situation where He was the answer to a need. For example, He declared, "I AM the Bread of Life" following the feeding of 5,000 hungry people. Then, a woman was about to be stoned to death when He said, "I AM the Light of the world.

The entire ninth chapter of John focuses on a man born blind whom Jesus healed. The Pharisees cast this man out of the synagogue because he was healed on the Sabbath day. Jesus responded to these leaders who had closed the door of their synagogue to this helpless man. He said, "I am the door of the sheep. All who came before Me are thieves and robbers, but the sheep didn't listen to them. I am the door. If anyone enters by Me, he will be saved and will come in and go out and find pasture" (John 10:7-9).

Jesus' hearers were well acquainted with sheep and their care. When He spoke of being the door of the sheep, they understood His meaning. Shepherds led their sheep out to pastures on the hillsides during the day. At night the caregivers needed a safe place for these helpless animals. Large round enclosures with low stone walls were available. Several flocks would be kept overnight in these pens. One small opening allowed passage for the sheep. A hired gatekeeper would lie across this opening at night, becoming the door. He kept the sheep safely inside and prevented thieves and robbers, as well as wolves, from taking the sheep.

When Jesus claimed to be the door of the sheep, He referred to the fact that He is the way for individuals to enter the safety of the kingdom of God. All who enter by trusting Him will be protected from Satan's destructive schemes. What a contrast between Him as an open door and the Pharisees who closed the door to this man who was so thrilled at being healed.

Notice a further reference to an "open door." John's visions of heaven, recorded in the Revelation, include these interesting words, "After this I looked, and there in heaven was an open door" (Revelation 4:1). The door of salvation is wide open. Jesus is that door in the sense that through His sacrifice on the cross He makes eternal life available to all who come to Him. Have you chosen to enter this door? Are you safe in His protective care? **Yeshua** saves!

I AM the good shepherd.

Sheep are among the most dependent, helpless creatures on earth. They desperately need a shepherd. So do we. How grateful we should be that **Yeshua** came to be our shepherd. Peter reminded his readers of this fact: "For you were like sheep going astray, but you have now returned to the shepherd and guardian of your souls" (1 Peter 2:25). Notice these two important terms: *shepherd* and *guardian*. Both words speak clearly of the care, guidance, and protection the Good Shepherd provides for His sheep.

Chapter Nine of this study featured *Yahweh Roi*, I AM the Shepherd. Our focus was on the personal care provided by Yahweh. Jesus echoed this truth in John 10 as He declared, "I am the good shepherd" (v. 11). In the verses following this statement we find these significant words repeated five times: "I lay down My life for the sheep." The truth He affirmed and reaffirmed was the fact that in order to save the lost from perishing, He came to die so they might not perish forever in hell but live. Paul wrote of this amazing truth in his letter to the Romans: "Christ died for the ungodly. For rarely will someone die for a just person . . . . But God proves His own love for us in that while we were still sinners Christ died for us" (Romans 5:6-8).

One aspect of this salvation is most strongly emphasized in this passage from John 10. Jesus promises that all who become his "sheep" will be given eternal life by Him. That is, He pledges to keep them from ever perishing. Bible teachers often referred to this truth as the doctrine of eternal security, popularly known as "once saved, always saved." Notice these words from the Good Shepherd: "My sheep hear My voice, I know them, and they follow Me. I give them eternal life, and they will never perish—ever! No one will snatch them out of My hand. My Father, who has given them to

Me is greater than all. No one is able to snatch them out of the Father's hand. The Father and I are one" (John 10:27-30).

The grammatical construction of this passage is interesting. If a person speaking Greek wanted to emphasize a negative statement, he would use two different negative terms together. In verse 28 Jesus literal words are: "I give them eternal life, and they will *not never* perish." Here is a very strong expression of a salvation that is eternally secure. With Jesus as our Good Shepherd we never, ever, need to fear that some one or some thing might take us from His care and cause us to perish.

I AM the resurrection and the life.

This remarkable statement was made by Yeshua at another need-meeting situation. His friends Mary and Martha were grieving over the death of their brother Lazarus. Four days earlier they had sent for Jesus to come and heal their brother. After deliberately waiting this long, Jesus arrived to comfort these dear friends. These sisters expressed disappointment that He had come too late to help Lazarus.

The most hope-filled words of comfort were spoken to them by Jesus. He boldly announced, "I am the resurrection and the life. The one who believes in Me, even if he dies, will live. Everyone who lives and believes in Me will never die—ever" (John 11:25-26). Notice another double negative "never die—ever." Here is an incredible promise to make, especially regarding a man who had been dead and buried for four days!

Jesus proceeded to the burial site where He called Lazarus to come forth. To the absolute amazement of everyone present, Jesus' friend appeared, still wrapped as a corpse. Jesus' final command is interesting: "Loose him and let him go" (v. 44). What a unique and awesome miracle! We read of other occasions when Jesus revived someone who had recently expired, but never a person who had been dead and buried this long.

Can you grasp the clear message Jesus conveyed through this amazing event? Certainly His compassion for those in sorrow is obviously revealed. But far more significant is this example of His authority over death. Paul expressed this fact in his words to Timothy, "Our Savior **Christ Jesus . . . has abolished death** and has brought life and immortality to light through the gospel" (2 Timothy 1:10).

The death of our physical body occurs, but not the death of our soul and spirit, the real person we are. A believer's death is a spiritual liberation from the physical body. Those who place their trust in **Yeshua** "never die—ever." Again, quoting Paul, "For we walk by faith, not by sight—yet we are confident and satisfied to be out of the body and at home with the Lord" (2 Corinthians 5:7-8). **The ultimate goal of salvation is our total and final deliverance from death and the grave, along with the joy of being in heaven with our Redeemer.**

> *The ultimate goal of salvation is our total and final deliverance from death and the grave, along with the joy of being in heaven with our Redeemer.*

This physical body will also be resurrected at the return of Jesus. Paul addressed this issue in 1 Corinthians 15. He was speaking of the resurrection of our bodies when he wrote: "This corruptible [human body] must be clothed with incorruptibility, and this mortal [human body] must be clothed with immortality. Now when this corruptible is clothed with incorruptibility, and this mortal is clothed with immortality, then the saying that is written will take place: Death has been swallowed up in victory . . . . thanks be to God who gives us the victory through our Lord Jesus Christ!" (1 Corinthians 15:53-57).

The story is told of an old soldier who said, "When I die do not sound 'Taps' over my grave, but 'Reveille' the morning call, the summons to rise!" How fitting this sound would be for all who know Him, who is the Resurrection and the Life.

I AM the way, the truth, and the life.

These words of Jesus actually repeat what He said earlier. As the Door, He is **the way** to salvation. As the Light of the World, He is **the truth**. As the Resurrection, He is **the life**. He obviously felt the need to restate these words due to the situation at hand.

The occasion for this triple claim is found in John 13:21—14:11. Jesus made several statements that caused His disciples to be very troubled. First, He announced that one of them would betray him (13:21). Then He told them He was going away and they could not follow Him at that time

(13:36). Moreover, He told Peter that before the next daybreak he would deny Jesus three times (13:38).

Imagine the anguish felt by these disciples as Jesus informed them of what was coming. He sought to bring comfort, especially to Peter, by speaking to him these familiar words of comfort, "Your heart must not be troubled. Believe in God; believe also in Me. In My Father's house are many dwelling places, if not, I would have told you. I am going away to prepare a place for you. If I go away and prepare a place for you, I will come back and receive you to Myself, so that where I am you may be also. You know the way where I am going" (14:1-4).

Upon hearing these words, Thomas replied, "Lord, we don't know where You're going. How can we know the way?" (14:5) Jesus answered this sincere question by stating, "I am the way, the truth, and the life. No one comes to the Father except through Me" (14:6). Let's examine each of these claims separately in the light of the occasion in which they were first spoken.

"I am the way" is Jesus' clear answer to Thomas' question: "How can we know the way?" Jesus had just indicated that He was leaving the disciples and going back to His Father. Although He made clear the fact that they could not accompany Him at that time, He wanted to reassure them of a future with Him in the Father's house. How could they get there? Jesus did not say that He would show them the way, but that **He is the way.** Only Jesus is the way to the Father because He alone became the sin-bearer for all who believe on Him. The writer of the Book of Hebrews refers to Jesus as our "intercessor," a term that literally means to plead on behalf of another. "Therefore He is always able to save those who come to God through Him, since He always lives to intercede for them"(Hebrews 7:25). Notice this phrase, "He is always able to save those who come to God through Him." Jesus is the way!

"I am . . . the truth." The context for these words suggest a specific meaning. The subject of Jesus' discourse is God the Father. He began by referring to the fact that God would be glorified through Jesus (13:31-32), Jesus was finally going to His Father's house, "No one comes to the Father except through Me" (v. 6). Although Jesus is the truth about everything that relates to life, in this instance He refers to *truth about God.* Notice how Philip said, "Lord, show us the Father, and that's enough for us"

(14:8). Jesus replied, "Have I been among you all this time without your knowing Me, Philip? The one who has seen Me has seen the Father . . . . Believe Me that I am in the Father and the Father is in Me" (vv. 9-11). **All the truth a person ever needs to know about God is found in Jesus.** He is the truth about God.

"I am the life." Eternal life is more than a duration, living forever—for eternity. Eternal life is a special kind of life, the very life of God. Jesus is the life of God made available to all who choose to believe and receive Him. John made this truth very clear in these simple words, "God has given us eternal life, and this life is in His Son. The one who has the Son has life. The one who doesn't have the Son of God does not have life" (1 John 5:11-12). **Eternal life is obtained, not by what a person achieves, rather by Who a person receives. Jesus is the life, eternal life.**

You may ask, How can I receive Him? Again, the answer is clearly expressed in these words, "Listen! I stand at the door and knock. If anyone hears My voice and opens the door. I will come in to Him . . . ." (Revelation 3:20). We open the door by choosing to offer a prayer like this: Lord, Jesus, I believe that You are the Son of God, who died to pay the penalty for my sins and rose from the dead to be my life. I turn from myself and my sinful ways to ask You to come into my heart as my Savior and Lord. I give myself to You. Amen.

Thomas a Kempis, the fifteenth century writer put these truths together in a very memorable manner when he said,

"Without the way, we cannot go;

Without the truth, we cannot know;

Without the life, we cannot live."

I AM the vine.

Jesus' disciples, who first heard these words, were very familiar with vineyards. In fact, they may have been passing near vineyards when He called their attention to the vine-branch-fruit imagery. They understood the importance of grape branches staying firmly attached to the vine in order to produce fruit. In addition these followers recognized the necessity of unfruitful branches being removed through pruning.

With all this background information in mind, Jesus did a masterful job of using what was familiar to teach what His disciples needed to understand about their relationship with Him. His reason for choosing this particular time for such a special lesson may have been the fact that He would soon be arrested, beaten, and crucified. The True Vine faced severe pruning. Some branches would be removed so others could bear more fruit.

Let's get the picture. Jesus is the vine; believers are the branches. The Vine produces fruit through the branches if they remain closely attached. The Father is the vineyard keeper who prunes the vine to increase the fruit.

Jesus gave this illustration in order to emphasize the importance of maintaining a close, vital relationship with Him. Eleven times in John 15:1-17 He used the word *remain*. If disciples are to be fruitful, they must guard their connection to Jesus—remaining in close fellowship with Him. Apart from Him, they could do nothing in the sense of producing fruit. What is required of those who want to "remain" in Him? Jesus gives the answer in these words, "As the Father has loved Me, I have also loved you. Remain in My love. If you keep My commands you will remain in My love, just as I have kept My Father's commands and remain in His love" (John 15:9-10).

The word translated "remain" is sometimes rendered as "abide" or "continue." Jesus was saying that if a person is committed to obeying the command to love God and love all others, that individual will remain in a strong fellowship with Him. The result will be that of bearing much fruit (v. 5).

What is this fruit? The fruit of any vine is determined by the nature of that vine. This vine is Jesus, and thus the fruit is a person who bears His likeness. Another expression of this truth is found in Paul's words concerning "the fruit of the Spirit." In His letter to the Galatian churches, he wrote, "The fruit of the Spirit is love, joy, peace, patience, kindness, goodness, faith, gentleness, self-control" (Galatians 5:22). Notice that these virtues are not nine separate *fruits;* rather they are nine characteristics of *one fruit.* The Spirit of Christ in a believer will seek to produce the character and person of Christ through that person.

In other words, Jesus as the Vine produces Jesus-like fruit—persons who bear His likeness.

Consider one final truth from this passage in John 15. Jesus said of this teaching regarding the vine-branch-fruit, "I have spoken these things to you so that My joy may be in you and your joy may be complete" (v. 11). Here is the joy of salvation, the joy of being delivered from sin to become a Christ-like person. Jesus' purpose for us is not that we become some solemn faced, adherent of an unpleasant, burdensome, rule-keeping cult. Rather, He came to set us free from all that would hinder a joy-filled daily walk with Him. As Paul exclaimed, "Rejoice in the Lord always. I will say it again, Rejoice! (Philippians 4:4).

I AM the first and the last, and the Living One.

The revelation of this title goes all the way back to Isaiah 41: 4, "I, Yahweh, am the first and with the last –I am He." The same expression occurs in Isaiah 44:6, and 48:12.Then **Yeshua** makes the claim for Himself four times in the Revelation, adding the Greek letters to state, "I am the Alpha and the Omega, the One who is, who was, and who is coming, the Almighty" (Revelation 1:8, 17; 21:6; 22:13).

Alpha and omega are the first and last letters of the Greek alphabet. Thus Jesus claimed to be the first and the last, the beginning and the end. **He is like the bookends of history. All creation began with Him and all human history will end with Him.** This truth is a strong affirmation of Yahweh's sovereignty.

Earlier in this chapter we spoke of *Yeshua* meaning "I AM the One who saves." The terms *alpha* and *omega* are used here to declare the fact that He is the beginning and the end, not only of history but also of salvation. Apart from Him salvation would not be possible; neither would anyone experience deliverance from sins and their consequences.

One Bible teacher has said, "Jesus is the beginning and the end, and everything in between!" Indeed, He is everything, from the beginning to the end, of personal salvation. **Yeshua** begins saving us with a new birth, then concludes salvation by receiving us to heaven. However, He also continues saving us all the way along the path of life. You may be familiar with a gospel tract entitled, "The ABCs of Salvation." This witnessing tool gives three, easy-to-remember steps to being born again. However, there is far more to salvation than these ABCs. Yeshua provides all we need from A all the way through Z!

I AM the ROOT and the OFFSPRING of David, the Bright Morning Star

Among the final words of Jesus given in the Bible is this solemn claim found in Revelation 22:16. Here is the final I AM statement. But notice, rather than being the end, the "morning star" heralds the arrival of a new day!

Examine these interesting, revealing terms more closely. A "root" is the hidden part of a plant and its source of life. David and all his descendants were created by the Lord Jesus. This metaphor is an expression of the *divine* nature of **Yeshua**. He produced the family tree of David, just as a root produces any plant.

"The offspring of David" is an Old Testament reference to the promised Messiah. Listen to these words from Yahweh to David regarding that covenant: "Yahweh Himself will make a house for you. When your time comes and you rest with your fathers, I will raise up after you your descendant who will come from your body, and I will establish his kingdom . . . . Your house and kingdom will endure before Me forever, and your throne will be established forever" (2 Samuel 7:12-16). Psalm 89 adds clarity to this promise: "Once and for all I have sworn an oath by My holiness; I will not lie to David. His offspring will continue forever, his throne like the sun before Me, like the moon, established forever, a faithful witness in the sky" (Psalm 89:35-37). These promises refer to the *humanity* of Jesus, a blood descendant of David, through his mother Mary. **Thus the Bible closes with a strong affirmation of the divine/human nature of our Savior.**

In biblical times the astronomers considered that bright object in the pre-dawn sky to be a star. We know this light to be the planet Venus, reflecting the light of the sun, much as our moon. Venus often appears just before dawn to herald the beginning of a new day. Likewise, **Yeshua came to usher in a new beginning**. As John wrote, "I saw a new heaven and a new earth, for the first heaven and the first earth had passed away, and the sea existed no longer. I also saw the Holy City, new Jerusalem, coming down out of heaven from God . . ." (Revelation 21:1-2).

I am coming quickly.

Although this is not the same *I AM* construction in the Greek language as the others, still **Yeshua's final recorded words are, "Yes, I am coming quickly."** John responds to say, "Amen, Come, Lord Jesus!" (Revelation 22:20). [Paul expressed a similar plea in his concluding words to the church in Corinth, *"Marana tha* that is, Lord, come!" (1 Corinthians 16:22)]. So **the Bible ends with the promise of a new beginning.** Each of us must face and answer the question: Am I ready to meet Him, whether in the air (rapture) or when He calls me through death? Now is the only time I have for certain to get ready. How interesting that among the final words of the Scripture is this appeal, "Both the Spirit and the bride say, 'Come!' Anyone who hears should say, 'Come!' And the one who is thirsty should come. Whoever desires should take **the living water** as a gift" (v. 17).

This last phrase reminds us of Jesus' words to the woman at the well in Samaria. As part of their discussion, He said, to her, "If you knew the gift of God, and who is saying to you, 'Give Me a drink,' you would ask Him, and He would give you **living water**. . . . Everyone who drinks from this water will get thirsty again. But whoever drinks from the water that I will give him will never get thirsty again—ever! In fact, the water I will give him will become a well of water springing up within him for eternal life" (John 4:10-14).

A river of **living water** flows all the way through God's Word. Yahweh, Himself, is this river. Notice this flow of life beginning with the first mention of Yahweh found in Genesis 2:4, ". . . Yahweh God made the earth and the heavens." *Yahweh* is the most commonly used noun of the entire Old Testament, occurring there 6,828 times. The New Testament opens with an angel giving Joseph the name of his son—**Yeshua** (Yahweh is salvation). Over 700 more references to Yahweh by this new name occur in the New Testament. The Bible is all about Him!

Yeshua said on one occasion, "If anyone is thirsty, he should come to Me and drink! The one who believes in Me, as the Scripture has said, will have streams of **living water** flow from deep within him" (John 7:37-38).

The stream flows on through each person who receives Him. We drink of this life-giving stream, but we must not seek to contain it. His life flows in us and through us out to refresh others. How exciting to know the pleasure of being a channel of this **living water!**

What a difference this name makes—Yeshua, I AM salvation. A salvation from A to Z, and everything in between! Apart from Him we would all be condemned because of our sin. We would face eternity apart from God, apart from heaven and all who are there, and apart from hope.

Suggested prayer: **Bless Yeshua O my soul and all that is within me, bless His holy name. How eternally grateful I am for all You have done to provide salvation for me. You have given Yourself to set me free from the bondage of sin and the condemnation I deserve. You are my life, my joy, my peace, and the rock of my salvation.**

I claim Your resources of grace to become all you have saved me to be. May the radiance of Your life be revealed through all I do and think and say. Let Your living water flow out of me to everyone in my family, my friends, my neighbors, and all I meet.

Bless Your holy name, even Yeshua Messiah, King of kings and Lord of lords. Amen.

STUDY GUIDE

Chapter 12: The Difference Between Salvation and Condemnation

1. Why should anyone be concerned about eternal condemnation?

2. What personal needs are included in the biblical concept of salvation?

3. Explain the connection between these names: Jesus, Joshua, and Yeshua.

4. Which of the nine "I AM" statements of Yeshua is most meaningful to you? Why?

CHAPTER THIRTEEN

What Personal Differences His Name Makes

A MISSIONARY KID, WHO grew up in Trinidad, tells the story of a memorable time when Queen Elizabeth came to their town on a visit. His father held him high enough to see the entire parade. First came the high school band, followed by marching soldiers and guards mounted on horses. Local dignitaries rode by, seated on the back of convertibles. Then came the queen in her limousine with armed guards walking alongside. Her highness waved a white handkerchief to the cheering crowds of her loyal subjects.

However the celebration was short-lived. The entourage moved on and life in the town returned to normal. The boy's descriptive words were, "Royalty came to town but nothing really changed!" How true of most personal events. Real life-changing experiences rarely occur. **The thesis of this book is that when Yahweh is understood and enthroned in one's heart, everything changes!** He makes a profound and eternal difference on a personal level. We are never the same after truly knowing *Yahweh*.

> *The thesis of this book is that when Yahweh is understood and enthroned in one's heart, everything changes!*

The Bible reveals various combinations of His Name that clearly describe these changes. This concluding chapter gives help by defining four specific aspects of life where these significant differences are most powerfully experienced.

1. **Our worship of Yahweh is enriched.** Archaeologists have discovered that the most ancient primitive people groups were worshipers. Each had

their own gods who were recognized and honored in various manners. All humankind is created in the image of God. Therefore **our basic nature is to acknowledge and worship some expression of a higher power.** Unfortunately, sin has so corrupted man's understanding of God that most cultures bow down to false gods, worshiping in ways that are often destructive as well as unfulfilling.

Jesus gave one of the most helpful insights regarding worship when He told a sinful woman, **"God is spirit, and those who worship Him must worship in spirit and truth** (John 4:24). These words help us understand that authentic worship is a spiritual experience. Worship is not primarily a matter of our being in some special place, such as a church building. Nor does genuine worship entail various rituals and ceremonies. Worship is spiritual, the response of our human spirit to the Spirit of God. One worship leader defines worship as: "Our whole life response to God's revelation of Himself to us." This response must be according to **truth**—the truth about who God is and what pleases Him. **The quality of our worship will be in direct proportion to our understanding of the God we worship.**

God has chosen to make Himself known in various ways. Theologians refer to natural revelation and special revelation. Natural revelation includes all the truth about God that can be learned through nature, namely His creative power, wisdom, and beauty. Who of us has not been moved to praise God as the result of a beautiful sunset, or a pastoral scene, or the fine features and fragrance of a flower, or the wonder of a new born child?

Special revelation comes primarily through the Bible. As the psalmist declared, "The revelation of Your words brings light and gives understanding to the inexperienced" (Psalm 119:130). The book you are now holding in your hands gives special attention to Yahweh's name and those combinations of His name that occur throughout the Bible. These meaningful terms have enriched the worship of those who knew them. One example is found in Gideon's worship experience when he made an altar, naming it *Yahweh Shalom*, "I AM the One who gives peace" (Judges 6:23-24). His worship had special meaning because he had just experienced the peace Yahweh gives. My personal testimony is that knowing these expressions regarding who God is has greatly enriched my worship of Him.

We can feel some kinship with Isaiah and his most meaningful experience of worship, recorded in Isaiah 6:1-13. He had a vision of Yahweh in which angels declared, "Holy, holy, holy is Yahweh Sabaoth" (v. 3). This amazing revelation made a profound impact upon this prophet. He was never the same. **Yahweh Sabaoth** may be translated "I AM the Lord of Hosts." This revelation of God's sovereignty came to Isaiah at a time of national crises. King Uzziah had died and the nation was threatened by the Assyrians. What would happen to them? Yahweh calmed Isaiah's fears by revealing Himself as the One who was greater than all human powers (**Yahweh Sabaoth**). What a meaningful time of worship for this servant!

You may have never been in this kind of dilemma, but you can experience the comfort and reassurance that knowing God as **Yahweh Sabaoth** can make. My most meaningful times of worship have occurred through praying the various name combinations found in this book. Follow this example of the way these terms become expressions of praise and gratitude.

> **Yahweh,** I bow in worship before You because You alone are the One who always IS. Thank you for revealing Yourself to us as **Yahweh Yireh**, the One who provides whatever we need. Our first need is for complete healing, physically, emotionally, relationally and spiritually. **Yahweh Rophe** You have met that need completely.
>
> We praise You as **Yahweh Nissi** for giving us victory over every adversary. You also are faithful as to set us apart as one belonging to you as **Yahweh M'Kaddesh.** All these blessings have given us that special peace that **Yahweh Shalom** alone can supply. I bow in wonder and amazement that You would declare such a sinner as I to be righteous before You—You are **Yahweh Tsidkenu** indeed.
>
> How wonder-filled we are to know you as **Yahweh Shammah**, the One who is always present. Your care for us as **Yahweh Rohi**, our shepherd, brings lasting security and joy. My gratitude overflows as I contemplate Your greatness as **Yahweh Sabaoth**, the LORD of Hosts.

All praise belongs to **Adonai Yahweh**, as the One who is sovereign over me now and forever.

Holy **Yeshua**, You indeed have provided all the spiritual nourishment we need as our **Bread of Life**. We are blessed to no longer walk in darkness but to have You within us as the **Light of the World**. Thank You for being **the Door** through which we have entered the kingdom of God. We find such security in knowing You as our **Good Shepherd** who daily protects us from all enemies. I continue to worship You for giving me the assurance that when the time comes for me to pass from this brief life, I will not die because You are there as **the Resurrection and the Life**.

We celebrate all You mean to us as **the Way** to God, **the Truth** about God, **and the Life** of God. Praise belongs to You as **the Vine** who upholds us and produces much good fruit through us as Your branch. Yes, You are my **Alpha and Omega**, the First and the Last. I worship you as the One who is my beginning and ending, just as You were **the Root and Offspring of David**. How thrilled I am to know that all the past and present is but a prelude to the glorious New Day that you herald as **the Bright Morning Star!** All these blessings provoke the deepest and strongest expression of worship I will ever know. Thank You. Amen.

Readers will notice that these terms are given in order of their occurrence in this book and in the Bible. **I am convinced that a divine design is in this order**. A plan that makes these terms all the more meaningful. You are encouraged to make this prayer a model for your own special times of worship. You will never be the same. I challenge you to discover a new dimension to your personal, private worship through use of these combinations. **His Name makes a profound and enriching difference in our worship.**

2. Our walk with Yahweh is improved. You have probably heard this saying: "A Christian's walk and talk should agree; he should walk the talk." What this expression implies is that **there should be no difference between what we claim to *believe* and the way we *behave*.** Paul referred to this truth when he said to his readers, "As you have received Christ

Jesus the Lord, walk in Him, rooted and built up in Him and established in the faith, just as you were taught, and overflowing with thankfulness" (Colossians 2:6).

Walking with Yahweh means to have a close, intimate fellowship with Him. From the beginning of creation such personal communion has been His plan. Genesis 3:8 speaks of Adam and Eve hearing "the sound of Yahweh God walking in the garden at the time of the evening breeze." Apparently He was accustomed to walking together with this first couple. As the text reads, "Yahweh God called out to the man and said to him, 'Where are you?'" They had hidden themselves because of their disobedience to His command. Their walk with Yahweh ceased due to their sin.

Later we read of both Enoch and Noah being men who walked with God (Genesis 5:24; 6:9). Such intimate fellowship is pleasing to God; however, He will not remain in fellowship with sin. As Yahweh said through the prophet Amos, "Can two walk together unless they are agreed?" (Amos 3:3 NKJV). **Walking in fellowship with Yahweh requires agreement with Him**. We must agree that His way is best as we commit ourselves to obey to His commands and be surrendered to His will.

Jesus gave a very helpful metaphor regarding the nature of this intimate fellowship. He compared our relationship to Him as that of a vine and branch (John 15:1-17). As long as a firm union exists between a vine and branch, much fruit can be produced. He said, "I AM the vine; you are the branches. The one who remains in Me and I in him produces much fruit, because you can do nothing without Me" (v. 5). Understanding the implications of Yeshua as the Vine, can bring a big improvement upon our walk with Him.

You've heard the statement, "If it is to be, it's up to me." These words sound rather impressive and challenging. In fact most of us have bought in to this way of thinking much of our lives. We assumed that our shortcomings were the result of a lack of effort and persistence on our part. **The truth is—Christians can do nothing (that is pleasing to God) apart from Jesus working in and through us.** You may recall our study of Yeshua as the Vine and believers as the branches. He said, "I am the vine; you are the branches. The one who remains in Me and I in him produces much fruit, because **you can do nothing without Me**" (John 15:5). Paul clearly expressed the opposite, positive side of this truth when he wrote, "I am able to do all things **through Him** who strengthens me" (Philippians 4:13). **We are doing our best when we are relying on His best.**

Now return to the Vine/branch illustration. Yeshua is the One who produces the fruit through us as the branch. **Our focus is not to be on producing the fruit, rather on the connection to the Vine.** As we learn to abide in Him, through obedience to Him, the fruit will appear—in abundance. What an improvement over the result of just doing our best!

Listen to these encouraging words: "Yahweh is the everlasting God, the Creator of the whole earth. He never grows faint or weary; there is no limit to His understanding. He gives strength to the weary and strengthens the powerless. Youths may faint and grow weary, and young men stumble and fall, but those who trust in Yahweh will renew their strength; they will soar on wings like eagles; they will run and not grow weary; **they will walk and not faint**" (Isaiah 40:28-31).

3. Our work with Yahweh is enlightened. The terms we have considered that describe Yahweh not only shed light on *what* He is doing but also *where* He is doing these mighty acts. You will remember the title, *Yahweh Shammah*—I AM the One who is always present. The reality of His inescapable presence is one of the most meaningful of His attributes. Jesus promised, "Remember, I am with you always, to the end of the age" (Matthew 28:20). Many other similar statements can be cited, such as "I will never leave you or forsake you" (Hebrews 13:5). A relevant question is: Do we believe such promises? If we truly believe His promise to always be with us, never to leave us, why do we pray like this: Lord, please *be with me* today or Lord, *be with us* in this worship service today?

Such prayers are what I call prayers according to tradition. We have heard this kind of praying so often by so many church leaders that we just assume this is the way to pray. Would it not be better to offer prayers *of faith*, prayers that *affirm His promises*, such as Lord, thank You that You *are with us*; thank You for the assurance that *You will never leave us?*

What a tremendous difference is experienced when we become enlightened by the fact that no matter what we seek to do in serving Him, He is with us. Not only does He promise to be with us, but listen to these words, "It is God who is working **in** you, [enabling you] both to will and to act for His good purpose" (Philippians 2:13). "I labor for this, striving with His strength that works powerfully **in** me" (Colossians 1:29). Yeshua is always *with us* and always *working in and through us* to accomplish His purposes. Amazing!

Let's pursue this wonderful truth a little further. Paul's writings include several impressive benedictions. Notice the wording of this one: "Now to Him who is able to do above and beyond all that we ask or think—according to **the power that works in you**—to Him be glory in the church and in Christ Jesus to all generations, forever and ever. Amen" (Ephesians 3:20-21). The "power that works in you" is the Spirit of Christ, the Holy Spirit, who indwells every believer. As we seek to serve Yahweh, **what a difference is made by the awareness that nothing less than divine power is working in and through us.** No wonder Paul exclaimed, "I am able to do all things **through Him** who strengthens me" (Philippians 4:13).

This divine/human partnership may be expressed in many kinds of actions. Let's focus on one basic aspect of our work with Yahweh. Since He is the One working through us, we should expect this work to be much like the kind of work we see Him doing in the gospel accounts of His life. Listen to these statements Jesus made regarding His purpose for coming: ". . .the Son of Man did not come to be served, but to serve, and to give His life—a ransom for many" (Matthew 20:28). ". . . I am among you as the One who serves" (Luke 22:27).

Jesus, the greatest person to ever set foot on this earth, saw Himself as a servant to others. All the combination name/titles we have studied in this book reveal various ways in which He serves humankind. **His primary reason for working in and through us is to continue this role of helping others, of being their servant.** Our greatest sense of fulfillment comes as we join Him in this servant role. We are co-laborers with Yeshua as He reaches out to make a difference in the lives of others through us.

As a young pastor I had a learning experience that remains with me to this day. Our church building needed some additional classrooms, so we hired a local carpenter and I became his helper. Soon I noticed a saying he often repeated. As we cut sheets of wallboard to cover the new walls, some pieces did not fit perfectly. Often he would say, "Well, it's good enough for who it's for, nail it." Obviously, his determination of the quality of his work depended on "who it's for." His work ethic bothered me some since he was a Methodist doing the work for us Baptists!

That statement has stayed with me through these many years. **"Make it good enough for who it's for."** Since all we do should be for Jesus, we ought to be committed to making it our very best, that is, the best we can do through His wisdom and power. As Paul said, "Whatever you do, do it enthusiastically, as something **done for the Lord** and not for men, knowing that you will receive the reward of an inheritance from the Lord—you serve the Lord Christ" (Colossians 3:23-24).

The pastor of my hometown church, the First Baptist Church of Hobart, Oklahoma, is a fine young man named Keith Wiginton II. I quote from a recent article he wrote that impressed me.

"One of the most important choices you make every day is not the choice between right and wrong. That's important, but it's base level. The real choice is between **good** and **great**. Are you going to have a good marriage or are you going to have a great marriage? Are you going to settle for dating a good person or wait for a great person? Are you going to raise good little boys and girls or great men and women of God? Are you going to meet the minimum requirements at your job or are you going to set the standard with your greatness?

Unfortunately, it seems like most Christians never make the leap to that level. They stick to right and wrong, never realizing that **it's entirely possible to live a right life in a wrong way.** You could be a good person, but still live a shadow of the life God intended for you. **It's time for us to move past the good and move on to great!"**

What challenging truth! The awareness of His indwelling presence as **Yahweh Shammah** can give us the needed motivation to move from the good to the great. Knowing that He is always with us, working in and through us can literally transform the lowliest task from something commonplace and even dreaded into a service rendered by His power and for His glory. This fact can make all the difference between mere goodness to His greatness. Awesome!

4. Our witness of Yahweh is empowered. Every follower of Yeshua is called and commissioned to be His witness (Acts 1:8). The Greek term for *witness* is our English word "martyr." Thus a witness is one who lays down his or her life as a testimony. Yeshua referred to this sacrifice when He said, "If anyone wants to come with Me, he must deny himself, **take up his cross**, and follow Me. For whoever wants to save his life will lose it, but whoever loses his life because of Me will find it" (Matthew 16:24-25). **A cross is a place to die! We are called to be witnesses by becoming martyrs, that is, by laying down our lives for Him.**

You will notice in Jesus' invitation that the first step toward taking up our cross is to "deny" oneself. To deny means to say "no." If we want to successfully follow Jesus, we must begin by saying no to self and yes to Him—not my way, but His way. Such a radical, contrary-to-human nature decision requires more than personal determination. The old human, self-centered, self-gratifying nature does not die easily. In fact, this flawed, sin-corrupted aspect of every person remains as long as we live in this body. We must deliberately claim with Paul, "I have been crucified with Christ; and I no longer live, but Christ lives in me. The life I now live in the flesh, I live by faith in the Son of God, who loved me and gave Himself for me" (Galatians 2:20). The apostle gives us the secret to overcoming the old nature. Not by our best effort but "by faith" we claim His victory over being controlled by self.

This victory can be ours because *Yahweh Nissi* (IAM the One who overcomes) lives in us. **We actually have this source of victory over self and sin and the world present with us all the time. This awareness empowers us to be bold witnesses of Him**. A prayer that I often pray is this: "Yahweh, I ask that You use me to be a witness to everyone who comes to our house today." Often when a delivery person, such as a UPS worker, brings a package to us, I thank them and say, "You have been kind to me by bringing this, may I return the favor? The person always says yes. Then I ask if I may pray for them. Again, the response is positive. Often I ask if some personal need might be included in the prayer. Sometimes a genuine concern is shared. In my prayer I ask the Lord Jesus to bless this person, supply the answer to their need, and thank Him for hearing the prayer. Then if the person seems receptive, I may give some printed material regarding the way of salvation.

One sunny afternoon I was working in our front yard when a car turned in our drive way. A well-dressed man and woman got out and walked toward me. I could tell by their appearance and literature in hand that there were Jehovah Witnesses. Before they could say one word, I greeted them warmly and said, "I am glad you came. I am Yahweh's witness and I believe He brought you here so I can tell you about Him." Then I proceeded to share some of the truths recorded in this book, not giving them an opportunity to say anything. Finally I said, "Now, before you leave, I want to pray for you." As I reached out to lay my hands on their shoulders, they suddenly backed up, turned, got in their car and left! (I would like to have heard their report about this visit when they returned to their friends!)

I share this, not to make fun of these sincere individuals but to illustrate the fact that **knowing who Yahweh is will give a new bold confidence as we seek to be a witness of Him.**

The Old Mandola

When I think of **making a difference**, I remember an experience that began in my childhood and was most recently consummated. My uncle and aunt were farmers in southwest Oklahoma, not far from where our family lived. Visits to their home were always enjoyable. Although they never had children of their own, they made me feel like I was their very own son.

I remember seeing in a corner of their living room an old canvas case shaped like a large ukulele. Later I found out that this was a very fine musical instrument, an old (1903) Gibson mandola (kin to the mandolin). The case was never opened nor the instrument played when I was around. Years later after Val and I married, we occasionally visited this dear couple, and always came away with various food items that my aunt prepared for us. During our college days we enjoyed my aunt's frequent gifts of what she called "a box of old shoes" that turned out to be her homemade bread, jellies, canned vegetables, and other goodies.

Uncle Harry passed on and Aunt Mollie moved from their farm to our home town. She knew that Val was a fine musician so she gave us the old mandola. Since Val was more interested in other musical instruments like her accordion and piano, we left the mandola in its well-worn case. Years later we hung this gift on the wall near the piano. This valuable instrument became a conversation piece when guests came, but we never attempted to play it.

About two years ago I began thinking about all the great music that was buried in those old strings. I decided to explore the possibility of having the mandola restored and learning to play it myself. My friend Ron Shuff owns a local music store and referred me to a man who specializes in repairing stringed musical instruments. Upon examining the mandola, he was obviously very impressed and curious about its history. I told him all I knew about it as he prepared an estimate of his charges for restoration. The strings needed replacing and a small crack in the sound box had to be repaired. To my surprise he estimated its value at around $3,000!

Later Ron found a new case and arranged for a friend of his to give me a series of lessons on how to play this recently discovered treasure. My teacher was also impressed, not with my playing, but with the mandola. The lessons enabled me to play several basic chords. My first song to play seemed very appropriate, "Amazing Grace." Since then I've learned a few other songs and performed to the amusement of family and selected friends.

I see a parable of life in this old, damaged, useless, but restored instrument. In many ways, **we are all like this old mandola.** The Master Craftsman created each of us to make beautiful harmonies and bring pleasure to Him as well as to others. However, sin caused us to lose this original potential. We became damaged property, no longer capable of fulfilling our original purpose. However the Master Craftsman did not give up on His creation. He paid an enormous personal price as a means of restoration. Because of His love and by His amazing grace, all "old mandolas" can be restored. **We can be instruments in the hand of the Master Musician to produce beautiful music once more. What a difference He can make!**

Suggested prayer: **Gracious Master, You and You alone can make a lasting difference in me. Thank You for revealing Yourself as the divine Difference-Maker. Thank You for paying such a great and precious price to make these essential changes in me and in all who come by faith to You.**

You know that I cannot change myself. I trust you to take me as I am and make me whatever most pleases You. May there be a real and

lasting change in my worship of You, my walk with You, my work with You, and my witness about You.

My sincere desire is to be transformed by Your presence and power. I long to become all You desire for me to be.

Yeshua, You are life to me,
Giving peace and joy so free.
Guide me in Your perfect way;
Teach me just what I should say.
Use me as Your witness true;
Reveal Yourself in all I do.
Amen.

STUDY GUIDE

Chapter 13: What Personal Differences His Name Makes

Express the personal differences that knowing God as *Yahweh* makes in these areas of your life:

1. Your worship of Yahweh

2. Your walk with Yahweh

3. Your work with Yahweh

4. Your witness of Yahweh

BIBLIOGRAPHY

Arthur, Kay. *Lord, I Want to Know You*. Old Tappan, NJ: Fleming H. Revell Co. 1984.

Graham, Billy. *Peace with God*. Waco, TX: Word Books Publishing, 1984.

Goard, Wm. Pascoe. *The Names of God*. Muskogee, OK: Hoffman Printing Co. 2001.

Lockyer, Herbert. *All the Angels in the Bible*. Peabody, MA: Hendrickson Publishers, Inc., 2004.

Lockyer, Herbert. *All the Divine Names and Titles in the Bible*. Grand Rapids: Zondervan, 1975.

Lucado, Max. *Traveling Light*, Nashville, TN: Thomas Nelson, 2001

MacArthur, John. *Slave*. Nashville:Thomas Nelson. 2010

Morgan, Robert J. *He Shall Be Called*. New York: Warner Faith, 2005

Spangler, Ann. *Praying the Names of God*. Grand Rapids: Zondervan, 2004.

Stevenson, Herbert F. *Titles of the Triune God.* Greenwood, IN: Capstone Books, 2004.

Stone, Nathan. *Names of God.* Chicago: Moody Press, 1944.

Weisman, Charles A. *The Sacred Names Issue.* Apple Valley, MN: Weisman Publications, 2006

Wiersbe, Warren W. *The Wonderful Names of Jesus.* Wheaton, IL: Victor Books, 1980.

Commentaries, Dictionaries, and Encyclopedias Consulted:

Holman Bible Dictionary

Holman Bible Handbook

The Bible Exposition Commentary. Wiersbe, Warren.

The Broadman Bible Commentary

The Expositor's Bible Commentary, Edited by Frank E. Gaebelein.

The New American Commentary

The Encyclopedia Britannica

Lightning Source UK Ltd.
Milton Keynes UK

176971UK00001B/2/P